Richard Shepherd

The Ground And Credibility Of The Christian Religion

In A Course Of Sermons Preached Before The University Of Oxford

Richard Shepherd

The Ground And Credibility Of The Christian Religion
In A Course Of Sermons Preached Before The University Of Oxford

ISBN/EAN: 9783337087951

Printed in Europe, USA, Canada, Australia, Japan

Cover: Foto ©Lupo / pixelio.de

More available books at **www.hansebooks.com**

THE GROUND AND CREDIBILITY

OF THE

CHRISTIAN RELIGION:

IN

A COURSE OF

SERMONS

PREACHED BEFORE THE UNIVERSITY OF OXFORD,

AT THE

LECTURE

FOUNDED BY THE REV. JOHN BAMPTON, M. A. LATE CANON OF SALISBURY.

BY THE

REV. RICHARD SHEPHERD, D.D. F.R.S.
ARCHDEACON OF BEDFORD,
AND CHAPLAIN TO THE RIGHT REVEREND
THE LORD BISHOP OF DURHAM.

LONDON:
PRINTED FOR LOCKYER DAVIS, IN HOLBORN; AND
DANIEL PRINCE, OXFORD.
M,DCC,LXXXVIII.

Extract from the last Will and Testament of the late Rev. JOHN BAMPTON, *Canon of* Salisbury.

—— " I give and bequeath my Lands and Estates
" to the Chancellor, Masters, and Scholars of the
" University of Oxford for ever, to have and to hold
" all and singular the said Lands or Estates upon
" trust, and to the intents and purposes hereafter
" mentioned; that is to say, I will and appoint, that
" the Vice-Chancellor of the University of Oxford
" for the time being shall take and receive all the
" rents, issues, and profits thereof, and (after all
" taxes, reparations, and necessary deductions made)
" that he pay all the remainder to the endowment of
" eight Divinity Lecture Sermons, to be established
" for ever in the said University, and to be perform-
" ed in the manner following.

" I direct and appoint, that upon the first Tuesday
" in Easter Term, a Lecturer be yearly chosen by
" the Heads of Colleges only, and by no others, in
" the room adjoining to the Printing-House, between
" the hours of ten in the morning and two in the after-
" noon, to preach eight Divinity Lecture Sermons,
" the year following, at St. Mary's in Oxford, be-
" tween the commencement of the last month in Lent
" Term, and the end of the third week in Act
" Term.

" Also I direct and appoint, that the eight Divi-
" nity Lecture Sermons shall be preached upon either
" of the following subjects—to confirm and establish
" the Christian Faith, and to confute all heretics and
" schismatics—upon the divine authority of the Holy
" Scriptures—upon the authority of the writings of the
" primi-

"primitive Fathers, as to the faith and practice of the primitive Church—upon the Divinity of our Lord and Saviour Jesus Christ—upon the Divinity of the Holy Ghost—upon the Articles of the Christian Faith, as comprehended in the Apostles' and Nicene Creeds.

"Also I direct that thirty copies of the eight Divinity Lecture Sermons shall be always printed, within two months after they are preached, and one copy shall be given to the Chancellor of the University, and one copy to the head of every College, and one copy to the Mayor of the city of Oxford, and one copy to be put into the Bodleian Library; and the expence of printing them shall be paid out of the Lands or Estates given for establishing the Divinity Lecture Sermons; and the Preacher shall not be paid, nor be entitled to the revenue, before they are printed.

"Also I direct and appoint, that no person shall be qualified to preach the Divinity Lecture Sermons, unless he hath taken the Degree of Master of Arts at least, in one of the two Universities of Oxford or Cambridge; and the same person shall never preach the Divinity Lecture Sermons twice."

TO

THE RIGHT REVEREND

THOMAS THURLOW, D. D.

LORD BISHOP OF DURHAM.

MY LORD,

THE appointment, which produced the following Difcourfes, will in fome degree fanction my ambition to prefent them to the public under the protection of your Lordfhip's Name. It originated with the Univerfity of Oxford: and interefted as your Lordfhip is in whatever may claim

claim the least relation to a place, where you passed many of your early years with a Propriety of Conduct, that hath marked your Character through life, you will I am sure accept with Condescension the efforts thus excited, to elucidate the Truth and Purity of that Religion, of which you have ever discovered yourself in Heart and Practice a warm and consistent Friend.

I am well aware, that I have ventured on ground already taken; and that many valuable Treatises have appeared on the subject of the following sheets. But there is a mode of writing peculiar to different periods:

riods: and the Folios of the 'laſt age are ill reliſhed by the defultory readers of this. Hence it is, that fome of thofe publications alluded to have fallen into difeſteem; as being too diffufe, and appearing tedious: digreſſing into extraneous matter on fome points not very material, and treating with a degree of languor others of more importance. Thofe on the other hand, which are comprifed in the narrow limits of one or two Sermons, I conceive to be in fubſtance too compreſſed, to afford general fatisfaction; the Brevity requiring too many aſſumptions, to obviate the doubts of Sceptical enquirers. Others again, though recommending, and enforcing founded

Truths

DEDICATION.

Truths with Elegance and Perpicuity, feem rather calculated to imprefs the mind already perfuaded; than to obviate the Exceptions of Cavil, and fatisfy Scruple and Doubt.

These obfervations have long induced me to think fomething further wanting: fomething on the fubject in form and matter clear, yet clofe and argumentative; fuch as adverting to Objections as they rofe, and thus clearing the way to Truth, might command affent on the affured Ground of Conviction. Purfuant of fuch defign, I have, in the fubfequent inveftigation, taken nothing for granted: proceeding gradually from proof to proof, and

fhunshunning, as I proceeded, the discussion of no disputable article that lay in the way of my plan.

In those metaphysical disquisitions, to which my subject occasionally led me, I have particularly aimed at Perspicuity: sensible, that whenever a writer involves his ideas in Obscurity, it will always remain a doubt whether he be satisfactory to himself, and is an absolute bar to the conviction of others. On subjects of that nature, it is not easy to write to the comprehension of every reader; but, as far as I was able, I have attempted to do it.

DEDICATION.

And as new Adverſaries of a Religion, the Tenets of which are of a nature to excite none, but ſuch as are Adverſaries to human Happineſs, are continually aiming at new Objections, or vamping old ones up in new ſtile and figure; I have, on every article, more particularly applied myſelf to the Exceptions of modern writers. Every futile objection, in the ſhort form preſcribed on the preſent occaſion, it was not poſſible to notice: of thoſe that have been propoſed to the public with moſt Plauſibility, and retailed with the greateſt Succeſs, I have not deſignedly paſſed by any; for indeed I have obſerved none, that in the fair field of argument might not ſafely be met.

The

DEDICATION.

The plan I propofed to purfue, and which in the early Procefs of the Lectures I communicated to your Lordfhip, you were pleafed to regard in a favourable light: I have now to wifh the Execution may merit your equal approbation. But this in whatever degree your judgment may with-hold, I am eafy in the perfuafion, that your Lordfhip's known Zeal for the Interefts of our common Religion will with Candour regard a well-intentioned endeavour: a zeal, my Lord, which you have difplayed in every fituation of life; particularly in that exalted one, which afforded you the more ample fcope for exertion: not terminating there in cold and languid Wifhes, but exprefled expreſſed in a cordial Attention to indigent and deſerving Miniſters in your Dioceſe; who have often found themſelves promoted without Application on their Part, and often againſt the Application of Greatneſs and Power.

There is Merit in ſupporting an inferior Station with Firmneſs and Reſignation: but much greater, as it is a much more difficult part to ſuſtain, in filling an exalted one with Propriety and Attention; in which the Claims of Duty are more numerous, and the Charge of greater Weight. Our Minds indeed are formed with different Aptitudes: and ſome there are, that only feel themſelves in elevated Situations; where there is Scope for Exertion, and
Room

Room to expand. But it is your Lordship's peculiar Felicity, to appear formed, or more properly to form yourself, for every Situation in life, to which you have been occasionally called; from the literary eafe of academic privacy, to the highest honours of your profeffion: to have in every fituation, through which you paffed, conciliated Esteem, and left it with the general Regret of those, with whom you have been refpectively connected.

Those Inducements alone would have directed my pen to this Address, if more powerful ones were wanting: the Pleasure of acknowledging the Favours, I have from your Lordship myfelf received; and the Satisfaction

DEDICATION.

tisfaction of teftifying to the world, how much, and how truly, I have the Honour to be,

My Lord,

Your Lordfhip's dutiful,

Moft obliged,

And devoted fervant,

R. Shepherd.

ERRATA.

	Page
For *Practise* read *Practice*	7
—— *Weaknesses* read *Weakness*	92
—— *Man* read II. *Man*	96
—— *Diffidence* read *Diffidence*	139
—— *Sermon XI.* dele	160
—— *em* read *me*	166
—— *Reverence* read *Reference*	172
—— *lay* read *lie*	174
—— *and considered,* dele *and*	175
—— *nor do* read *neither do*	191
—— *Their Priests* dele	193
—— *Lic. de Divinatione* read *Cic. de Divinatione*	200
—— *termed* read *stiled*	216
—— προτοτοκος read πρωτοτοκος	232
—— *Resurection* read *Resurrection*	235
—— *them* read *them away*	271
—— *elucessens* read *elucescens*	280
—— *Tobrobanitarum* read *Taprobanitarum*	285
—— *hæe* read *hæc*	287
—— *affætaque* read *effætaque*	293

By the Author may be had,

Vol.
1. Miscellanies. Price 3s.
2. Letters on the Nature and Origin of Evil. Price 3s.
3. Reflections on the Doctrine of Materialism. Price 3s.
4. A free Examination of the Socinian Exposition of the Prefatory Verses of St. John's Gospel. Price 2s,

ADVERTISEMENT.

REFERENCE having been made in the Courfe of the following Difcourfes to a Paradifiacal State, the Author has annexed to them a Latin Sermon on the Subject; though written on a different Occafion, and preached feveral Years ago.

CONTENTS.

SERMON I.

Introductory Discourse, distinguishing the Excellency of Christianity from that variable Rule of Duty, in the Pretensions of moral Fitness held out by the Deist; and the Christianity of the Gospel, from that Species of it adopted by the Nazarenes and Ebionites, and by Socinus and his Followers revived.

PROV. iii. 13, &c.

Happy is the man that findeth wisdom, and the man that getteth understanding: &c.

SERMON II.

The Existence of God demonstrated: His Omnipotence, in the Supersedure of Nature, vindicated: His Immateriality asserted.

ROM.

Rom. i. 10, &c.

For the invisible Things of Him from the Creation of the World are clearly seen, being understood by the Things that are made; even His eternal Power and Godhead.

SERMON III.

A Divine Super-intendence displayed in the natural and moral Government of the World: establishing the Doctrine of a particular, as well as general, Providence.

Job. xxxi. 4.

Doth He noe see my ways, and count all my steps?

SERMON IV.

The general Obligation of Religion: the Ground and Necessity of the Duty of Prayer: the Connection between Religion and the social Duties.

Ps. xcv. 6.

O come let us worship and bow down; let us kneel before the Lord our maker: for He is onr God, and we are the People of His Pasture.

SERMON

CONTENTS.

SERMON V.

An Enquiry into the Competency of the Light of Nature, to afcertain the Duties of Religion; or whether a more exprefs Revelation of the Will of God in thofe Particulars be neceffary.

ISAIAH lix. 9.

We wait for Light; but behold Obfcurity: for Brightnefs, but we walk in Darknefs.

SERMON VI.

The Poffibility of a Revelation; and the Characteriftic marks neceffary to illuftrate it: with Confiderations on the Pretenfions of the Revelation made to the Jews.

JOHN iv. 2.

Salvation is of the Jews.

SERMON VII.

An Enquiry into the General Expectation of a Meffiah: and Whether the Prophetic writings of the Jews reprefent Him to have been a temporal Prince and Conqueror, or fomething greater.

MATT.

MATT. xxii. 42.
What think ye of Chrift?

SERMON VIII.

An Enquiry into the general Scope and Tenor of the Scriptures of the New Teftament, refpecting the Nature and Character of Chrift.

MATT. xxii. 42.
What think ye of Chrift?

CONCIO LATINA.
De Statu Paradifiaco.

ECCLUS. vii. 30.
Hoc tantum inveni; quod Deus homines perfectos creavit, ipfi autem ratiocinia plurima invenerunt.

THE
Ground and Credibility
OF THE
CHRISTIAN RELIGION.

SERMON I.

PROV. iii. 13, &c.

Happy is the man, that findeth wisdom, and the man that getteth understanding: for the merchandise of it is better than the merchandise of silver, and the gain thereof than fine gold. She is more precious than rubies, and all the things thou canst desire, are not to be compared with her. Length of days is in her right hand, and in her left hand riches and honour. Her ways are ways of pleasantness, and all her paths are peace. She is a tree of life to them, that lay hold on her.

THE original word חכמה, in this place rendered, wisdom, is, in the first chapter of this book of Proverbs, used in

SERMON I.

A the

SERMON I.

the plural number: which, according to the Hebrew idiom, is sometimes substituted for a superlative degree. *Wisdom crieth without*; or, literally translated, *wisdoms*: the word חכמות there denoting the highest and most excellent wisdom; the wisdom of religion: which is indeed so far the highest point of wisdom; that, though its roots be fixed on earth, its branches reach to heaven: it hath the promise both of this world, and that which is to come. 'Tis the same kind of wisdom, that is described in my text; and in this sense the word is frequently used, both in this book of Proverbs, and Ecclesiastes. The description is highly luxuriant; and were it as true, as it is rich and elegant, one might conceive it of such efficacy to captivate mankind; that no attention would be witheld, no exertions spared, to conciliate an ample plenary possession of her: at least that no wishes would prevail, no endeavours be exerted, to banish such a religion from the earth.

But

But with what religion will this engaging imagery comport? Not with the religion of nature; for in different ages, and different countries, the religion of nature hath deviated into the grossest errors. It taught the Persian, to pay his adoration to the sun; and some parts of India, to worship the tremendous power of darkness and evil. It directed the Egyptian, to fall down and humble himself to the reptile, and the plant; and impelled mankind to superstitions, often as immoral, as the rites themselves were ridiculous and vain. Whether the Theology of Greece and Rome were founded in political artifice, or in the flights of poetical imagination, the description before us can not apply to that religion: for it boasted not a single character of wisdom, purity, or satisfaction. Nor doth it aptly suit the imperfect, incompleat religion of the Jews. Burthened with a yoke of ceremonies, which, says the apostle, *neither we, nor our fathers were able to bear*; by a rigid observance of those ceremonies, exposed to innumerable and great hardships, and denied a variety of gratifications, did they tread the way of pleasantness: or cut off from the rest of the world, hating their neighbours, and in their turn despised and ridiculed by them, knew they the path of peace? The tree of life they had forfeited, and it had been removed far from them; nor did the institutions of their religion, nor even its promises, as understood by them, extend so far, as to enable them to lay hold on it.

The divine Encomiast looked farther, and higher. Rapt into future ages, he exhibits the picture of a perfect religion: and if we examine the traits of it, we shall find the animated description suit only the religion of Jesus Christ; and suit it in every particular. What is *the merchandise* of *silver* and *gold*, and *precious stones*, with all that is desirable in life; when set in competition with the gain, which that religion proposes, the

the acquisition of the Kingdom of Heaven? In enjoining temperance, the fountain of health, and parent of longevity, she holds out *length of days in her right hand*: and the general prohibition of sensual and worldly pleasures, *the lust of the flesh, the desire of the eye, and the pride of life,* which Christianity pronounces, will, if complied with, in its natural consequences, and according to the ordinary dispensations of Providence, conduct us to, what *her left hand offers, riches and honour.* So *easy is her yoke, and light her burden*; that her ways may be justly stiled *ways of pleasantness,* and *her paths the path-way of peace.* Through a Redeemer's sufferings, we are re-instated in the possession of *the tree of life:* and it is in every Christian's power, to reach out his hand, and *lay hold on it.*

If nature incline men to wish for happiness, and with the rules of such a religion as this, a religion so happily calculated to promote it, they cannot be brought

SERMON I. brought univerfally to comply; we have to lament the intemperance of youth, the worldly-mindednefs of age, and perhaps above all to deplore the known depravity of human nature, which can beft account for fo inconfiftent a conduct. But that numbers fhould be found, uninfluenced, as it may feem, by any incentive, except the fiend-like motive of counteracting the happinefs of the human race, anxious to extirpate fuch a religion from the world; now combating it with the force of arguments, fuch as fubtilty fupplies, now employing the light weapons of irony and ridicule againft it; haranguing difcipular circles in every place of public refort, retailing infipid objections, which have been a hundred times refuted, compaffing fea and land to make profelytes to their opinions: this, did not experience inconteftibly prove the fact, would tranfcend our belief; as it almoft baffles reafon to account for fuch exertions.

Some

Some motives however may be assigned, tending to excite those malevolent attacks: the affectation of singularity, the love of novelty, the repugnance to whatever checks the tide of present pleasures, the pride of seeming wise; the conscious meanness of acknowledging the charms of virtue, and at the same time stooping to the practise of vice, and, from thence derived, the audacity of justifying that practice by destroying or confounding all principles of religious truth. These, acting on different minds, may influence correspondent habits of thinking; and produce and explain the illiberal insults which religion sometimes sustains: while reason shudders at the desperate stake the rash adventurer risks in an unequal contest; where he can gain nothing, and may lose every thing.

SERMON I.

But amidst the various engines, that have been set at work, to prejudice the interests of Christianity, none are more mischievous

SERMON I.

mischievous than those; which have substituted some shew of religion in its room. For attacks upon a religion so pure in its precepts, so calculated to improve the mind in virtue, and raise it above mean, and selfish, and narrow pursuits, without the pretended introduction of some other religion in its place, can have no better effects with sober and serious men; than to convince them of secret designs, framed against virtue's self, and tending to set mankind loose from all restraints of conscience, and the shackles of moral duty.

Against such efforts the world is guarded: and treat them as desperate attempts to dissolve the bonds of society, and introduce barbarism, anarchy, and confusion. And that this must be the consequence of principles of Atheism, or of that kind of Theism, as detrimental to the morals of mankind as Atheism itself, which supposes God to have no regard of human actions, is a truth

truth generally assented to, and well understood.

Of those adversaries of Christianity, who advance with schemes of religion in their hands, I will mention only two. The one is he, who disclaims all revelation ; and bows down to the fantastic idol of moral fitness: an universal rule of action, as he represents it ; and in all instances a sufficient one, as he affects to believe it. Under the other character are understood those, who beneath the mask of Christianity employ their secret efforts against it : who insiduously assume its name, and scarcely that ;* who, while they say, Lord! Lord! are sedulously undermining that Lord's authority, dignity, and power. That advances against it, with the air and port of an open and avowed enemy : this enlists under its banner, only to

---

* In common with the Mahometans and Jews, the Socinians affect the appellation of UNITARIANS.

deceive ;

SERMON I.

deceive; thus employing againft it the double powers of hoftility and fraud: that bids bold defiance; this, like the falfe difciple, betrays with a kifs. We will examine the general features of each: their particular pretenfions will, in the courfe of the fubfequent lectures, be with more minutenefs inveftigated.

By thofe underminers of the Chriftian Faith, it will be obvious to my audience, that I have in my eye the fpawn of the antient Ebionites, the revived fect of the Socinians; whofe principal aim is not the denial of the Trinity, nor of the Divinity, nor Pre-exiftence of Chrift, nor of any other fingle article of Chriftianity: thofe may be fteps; but their mafked defign is an object of larger extent. Some diflike one gofpel, and fome another; and of thofe, which they admit, they hold themfelves at liberty to believe juft as much as they pleafe. They were firft ftiled Cerinthians, Ebionites, and Nazarenes: for thofe feveral fects, though

though differing in appellation, sprung up much about the same time, and in their fundamental doctrines were nearly the same. They acknowledged Jesus to have been the Messiah; but acknowledged him, with that defective apprehension of his nature and dignity, characterised by our Lord himself; *seeing they saw, but did not perceive; and hearing, they heard, but did not understand.* The uniform tenor of the gospel evinces a requisition of faith greater than the bare acknowledgment, that Jesus was the Messiah: his true disciples were further required to believe him to be the Son of God. Thus when our Lord asked them, whom they conceived him to be; Peter answered, *thou art Christ, the Son of the living God.* And at his trial the high priest in solemn terms adjured him to tell them, *whether he were Christ, the Son of God.* Hence we learn what was the true faith; and how far that of the Ebionites was defective. They admitted him to be the Messiah, but rejected the evangelical account of his

his Divinity: they pretended to believe him to have rifen from the dead, but allowed him no more than human powers.

Thofe were the the tenets, on which modern Socinianifm has been built: from its origin to the prefent day, a very contracted fect; and in the long fucceffion of feventeen hundred years continually dying away, and reviving. Paul of Samofate, bifhop and patriarch of Antioch, was their great luminary: with all the influence of his ftation, he propagated his doctrines; in which, finding himfelf refolutely oppofed, he with all the meannefs of a temporalift abjured them. The ftorm a little over, the reftlefs fpirit of innovation induced in him a fecond attempt to revive them: when the neighbouring bifhops affembled themfelves at Antioch; and, after a fair and candid difcuffion, unanimoufly condemned them: condemned thofe particular tenets, the denial of Chrift's Divinity, and of his

his defcent from Heaven. And the opinion, the whole Chriftian Church in that early age entertained of thofe tenets, forms a powerful argument againft them.

But I intend not in this difcourfe a Hiftory of Socinianifm; and therefore pafs over Theodotus, Symmachus, Artemon, and others; even the great Socinus himfelf, a man of fhrewd parts, but who wanted much the ballaft of learning: only remarking, that the doctrines, to which thofe Herefiarchs objected, themfelves plainly faw were founded on the exprefs word of fcripture; and therefore the fcriptures, fo afferting them, fome rejected, and others endeavoured to explain away. But it is not the rejection of this, or that fcripture doctrine, which will fatisfy our modern Socinians: with affected regard for Chrift, their brother, their teacher, and friend, they difown him as their Lord; and of his fupremacy. and original reject his own account:

Sermon I. account: with pretended zeal for Chriſtianity, their inceſſant labours are directed to undermine the authority of thoſe ſcriptures, on which Chriſtianity is founded.

Compared with modern Socinians, the more decent Mr. Toland purſues the ſame point with modeſty and moderation. All that he contends for is, the right of *interpreting ſcripture figuratively, when occaſion requires it.** We ſee, to what this will lead: for, every one judging for himſelf of the neceſſity of ſuch figurative interpretation, both doctrines and precepts will be eaſily interpreted away. Toland however keeps up a ſhew of reverence for the authority of the ſcriptures. But what ſay our modern Socinians? Why truly, that the " *pro* " *digious divine apparatus* of a particular " inſpiration of each ſacred writer [of " the Goſpels] was wholly unneceſſa-

---

* Chriſtianity not myſterious.

ry."*

" ry."* Of courſe it was not conferred, SERMON
or, in their own words, " this high I.
" notion of the inſpiration of the ſcrip-
" tures, of the Goſpel in particular, is
" contrary to fact."†

But though the goſpels were not dictated by particular inſpiration; " yet," ſays the author laſt quoted, " they may " be termed *in ſome degree* inſpired writ- " ings, as they contain a faithful detail " of the doctrine of Chriſt, which he " received immediately from God." Yes, admitting his repreſentation of them, they are juſt in ſuch degree inſpired, as other true hiſtorical details are. For, according to the account of Chriſt, which thoſe writers advance, where is the great difference between him and Socrates? They were both endowed by God with a greater degree of wiſdom, than other men poſſeſſed; for all wiſdom is from

* Prieſtley's Harmony of the Goſpels.
† Lindſey's Addreſs to the two Univerſities.

God:

God : neither of them left behind him any works of his own ; and the History of their Lives and Doctrines was each written by their respective disciples. The gospels therefore are just upon an equal footing of inspiration with the dialogues of Plato. And the religion, which instead of strict Christianity is under these refinements proposed, in its full extent amounts to these two points : the practice of the precepts of the gospel, as far as, considered in the light of a system of morals, we approve them ; and a belief of its doctrines, so far as we may judge, the Evangelists " had been care-
" ful to put down, with fidelity and
" exactness, what they had seen and
" heard themselves, respecting their *divine* master Jesus," (the denial of whose *divinity* by the bye is an especial tenet of the writer, I am now citing) " as also what they had learned from
" other competent witnesses."*

* Lindsey's Address, &c.

Here

Here we fee the defign fairly unfolded; which, as far as its influence may extend, muft weaken the obligation of the gofpel precepts, and effectually do its doctrines away : it fits thofe to every confcience, and invalidates the authority, that enforces thefe. Yet do the propagators of thofe tenets affume the title of Chriftians; open conventicles to the pretended honour of that Lord, whom they have thus degraded; and affect to form their religion on thofe fcriptures, they have robbed of the ftrongeft characteriftic of truth.

Such is the unfixt, variable fyftem of faith and morals, which the Socinian holds forth. The Deift, more candid, as more open, denies all revelation; and affects to own no other law, than that of nature. He pretends the foundation of his religion to be laid in reafon; and its rule of conduct to confift in the direction of that reafon, and the apparent aptitude and propriety of things. Moral

ral fitnefs, the object of his idolatry, beckons him to paths which fhe hath fhaped; and which, fhe promifes, the conduct fhe prefcribes will ftrew with flowers. She tells him, the fole end of man's exiftence here is, like that of the Leviathan in the deep, *to fport and take his paftime therein*; fhe bids him purfue and enjoy his own temporal happinefs; and, faving his own happinefs, to confult for, and promote, the happinefs of others. She addreffes him in the reprobated words of the apoftle; *eat and drink, for to morrow we die.* Enjoy the good things of this world, while they are in thy power; for this end were ye placed here, for this end were they given: and who knows what a day may bring forth.

Palatable reafoning this to the paffions and appetites of human nature: and captivating the religion; which on fuch eafy terms makes both worlds our own! For moral fitnefs, that meafures duty by the line of reafon, which again is regulated, or at leaft ftrongly influenced, by inclination,

inclination, will eafily perfuade her votary; that by employing his fuperfluities on objects in need, by dealing out his bread to the hungry, and cloathing the naked wanderer, he purchafes a licence to indulge himfelf in whatever practices his reafon, thus biaffed by appetite, may feem to fanction. He may laugh at fuperftition and indulgences: but were matters fairly and honeftly explained; it would be difficult to determine, in favour of which the divine voice of wifdom may decide.

The practice of a warm and diffufive benevolence is certainly a duty, highly incumbent on us to difcharge: yet are we not to lay the whole ftrefs of religion on it. Chriftianity reprefents it as only one part, and the inferior part too, of *the law and the prophets*: and reafon taught the heathen, that, apart from the focial and relative duties, there is a duty and fervice owing only, and immediately, to God. The duty of benevolence claims our regard, even as an act of religion; but not exclusively: it demands our observance; but not to the neglect of equally, or perhaps more, important ones. It is among the *things, which ought to be done*, but on account of which *others are not to be left undone.*

There is however a brilliancy, it must be acknowledged, in this fashionable religion; which is made to consist in a discrimination of moral rectitude, and a cultivation of the relative and social duties, particularly that of charity. It lays hold on our tenderest affections, it interests mankind in its favour, it *covers*, not compensates for, but conceals, or hides, *a multitude* of *sins.*

The passage just cited, men, whose religion sits easy on them, those good casuists, who would secure to themselves the next world, without giving up the pleasures of this, are very apt through ignorance to mistake, or misrepresent through

through defign: from thence alledging the fanction of fcriptural authority, to juftify a kind of commutation for fin. Whereas the apoftle's intention, in the ufe of the expreffion, being to inculcate the practice of brotherly love and charity, which our Lord and Mafter had particularly preffed upon his difciples, declaring it fhould be a badge of their difciplefhip, he makes ufe of that ftrong expreffion; only as intimating, that it was a virtue of fo bright and luminous a nature, as would attract the notice, and conciliate the good opinion of mankind, hiding by its luftre a multitude of little faults.

Take reafon, or revelation for your guide; and you will find both the one, and the other, inculcate our duty to God, as the firft and great duty: yet doth this favourite religion of the Deift, with all the focial virtues in its train, leave it entirely out of the queftion. " Quod " fupra nos, nihil ad nos;" is an apho-
rifm

rism ever in the mouth of those, who own no other religion than that. And thus, under the affectation of honouring the Deity by a distant humility, they are led to regard Him with indifference and neglect. "He is too elevated," reason they, "for us reptiles of a day "even in thought to approach him. "We are arguing in the dark, when "we dispute about his nature and at- "tributes: and without being acquain- "ted with his nature and attributes, we "cannot acceptably worship Him: but "not to worship Him acceptably and in "truth, is false religion: and false reli- "gion is worse than no religion at all."

But this fluent train of argument is false in every article. In giving us reason to discover that there is such a Being as God, our Creator hath declared it a duty to employ our thoughts on Him: and however little He hath been pleased to discover of Himself; that little it is the highest prerogative of our

nature

nature to look up to, and the moſt glorious exerciſe of the intellectual faculties to inveſtigate. Nor are we on this ſubject ſo much in the dark, as ſcepticiſm may pretend: want of demonſtration is no proof of falſhood; nor ought it to be any diſcouragement to the purſuit of truth. Without that perfect comprehenſion of the divine nature, which human preſumption may demand; it is aſſerted, that we may pay to our Creator a reaſonable ſervice: and it is denied, that a falſe religion is worſe than no religion at all. It may be ſo; but not neceſſarily. Conſidered in itſelf, and apart from the accidental malignity of its tenets, even a falſe religion is as much more acceptable to God, than no religion whatever; as an imperfect endeavour to pleaſe, is preferable to non-exertion and neglect. In a word, the knowledge of God, which, imperfect as it is, He hath ſtamped upon the human mind, ſufficiently evinces; that to contemplate Him, to acquaint ourſelves with Him, in order to inveſtigate how in the moſt acceptable manner to ſerve Him, is not above us: it is a duty incumbent on us; it produces in us a love of Him, and fulfils the firſt command.

If the excellent wiſdom of that full and perfect religion, which in doctrine and precept the goſpel exhibits, we contraſt with the two ſubſtitutes of it above deſcribed; we ſhall find it neither vague, nor defective. In reſpect of our duty to God, it teaches; that to *love him with all our heart, and all our ſoul, and with all our mind, and with all our ſtrength*; and agreeably to ſuch an inflamed, enlarged affection, to ſerve Him; is the firſt obligation of man. And for the regulation of our conduct to our neighbour, a proper diſcharge of the ſocial and relative duties, it lays down the completeſt rules in the ſhorteſt compaſs. " To love our neighbour, as ourſelves;" and " to do " to all men, as we would they ſhould " do unto us;" are maxims, that form the

the ground work of the best and com- pleteft fyftem of Ethics, moral philofo- phy ever framed.

SERMON I.

Its doctrines are authoritative and ex- prefs; its precepts clear and obligatory. However mens appetites, inclinations, humours, or caprice, may differ and va- ry; true religion will be always the fame: a perfect unchangeable rule of action. And though its precepts and doctrines we may pervert and wreft; we muft take heed, that in fo doing, we wreft them not to our own deftruction. Plain and fimple in its inftitution, it feeks no adventitious colourings; free from defects, it eludes not fcrutiny, nor fhuns the light: but the more we fee, and know, and are acquainted with it, the more defireable doth it appear to us.

Reafon is the touchftone, on which the truth of religion is to be tried. Let the Mahometan fay, BELIEVE: and guard the facred Koran from the fcru-
pulous

pulous eye of rational enquiry. Chrift hath faid, *fearch the fcriptures ; for they are they, which teftify of me.* And never have books been more critically, and more envioufly fearched, than they: while from thofe trials they have acquired new ftrength; rifing from the fiery ordeals with all the acquifition of luftre, trial and truth can give. The religion, which declines an appeal to the tribunal of reafon, is always to be fufpected. To her the Chriftian commits the guidance of his faith : her facred principles will fupport its authority, when from the faftidious countenance of Deifm the veil of prejudice fhall drop ; and the infidious fchemes of modern refiners fhall, like air-blown bubbles, float for their moment, amufe light minds, and die away : when unftable notions, and vain conceits, by wild imaginations fuggefted, and through love of novelty entertained, fhall by fober judgment be weighed, and in the cool hour of reflection relinquifhed. Schemes of religion, fuch such as these, may continue for a time; but, for want of a solid foundation, at length the baseless fabric must fall.

I. On these principles, in the discourses, which on the present occasion engage my attention, my design is, by a chain of arguments deduced from the foundation of all religion, the divine existence, summarily to evince the ground and credibility of the Revelation of Jesus Christ. In proof of that first great truth, the Being of a God, I shall have little occasion to dwell on arguments against the direct Atheist : the fool, who *says in his heart, there is no God.* I shall content myself therefore with advancing such only, as may be most satisfactory and convincing : and pass on 2dly to him, who, acknowledging the Being of a God, by a denial of miracles doth in effect limit his power ; a species of Anti-Theism scarcely less wicked, than direct Atheism itself. And I will 3dly advert to that more refined Atheist ;
whose

whose desperate principles of Materialism tend to degrade the Divine nature.

II. From the evidence of God's existence, we will proceed to the proofs of his superintending providence; a particular, as well as general, providence: that is, a providence, which not only directs and upholds the world in that ordinary course of nature, that succession of general causes and effects, which was in the first arrangement of things established; but such as with all-pervading eye observes, and guiding hand directs each lesser movement; every minute occurrence, as well as every extraordinary event.

III. And from these adduced proofs of God's existence and providence, I infer the duty of religion: that is, the proper acknowledgment of God's creative power, and upholding goodness, by acts of adoration and praise; obligatory

on

OF THE CHRISTIAN RELIGION. 29

on all beings endowed with a degree of reafon, equal to that of man.

SERMON
I.

IV. But though reafon be thus competent to point out the neceffity of religion; facts and experience evince its infufficiency to direct us aright in its doctrines and precepts, and the purity of worfhip: from whence follows the neceffity of a Revelation.

V. And on this fubject I fhall confine my thoughts to the nature and extent of the Revelation made to the Jews: the completion and perfection of which were deftined in the Meffiah..

VI. In examining the ancient prophecies of the Meffiah, my principal object will be to note and illuftrate thofe particulars, in which the Jews had miftaken and mifinterpreted them: not only in referring to worldly conquefts, pomp, and power, defcriptions, which with no human character could comport;

SERMON I.

port; but in their grofs mifapprehenfion of thofe prophecies alfo, which as plainly allude to his humiliated and fuffering ftate. And as thofe contrafting prophecies never did meet in any other of their great characters, nor ever can, but in one, who lived the life, performed the miracles, and experienced the fufferings, which Jefus did: they will not only demonftrate, that he was the Meffiah; but as affuredly prove, that he poffeffed powers more than human, and exercifed an authority, that marked his origin, as his miffion, divine.

VII. From the authorities of the Old Teftament, refpecting the nature and dignity of the Meffiah, I propofe to purfue my inveftigation of the fubject through the Scriptures of the New; and therein to enquire, 1ft, what is the general fcope, and uniform tenour of thofe fcriptures, refpecting the Pre-exiftence and Divinity of Chrift: and 2dly to meet the objections to thofe doctrines

in

in the full force, in which the leaders of a revived fect have preffed them. And in this inquiry may the fpirit of truth direct me, through Jefus Chrift our Lord : &c. &c.

SERMON

SERMON II.

Rom. i. 10, &c.

For the invisible things of Him from the creation of the world are clearly seen, being understood by the things that are made; even his eternal power and Godhead.

THE existence of God is so clearly manifested, and his creative power so far understood, saith the apostle; that even the Heathen are without excuse, in not paying Him that purity of worship, which his sublime nature and Godhead require. And indeed reason doth supply us with so cogent arguments of such a being, and those attributes of infinite power, wisdom and goodness, inseparable from Him, which St. Paul
stiles

ftiles " the invifible things of God"; as nothing but the moft determined prejudices can withftand.

SERMON II.

One would conceive that we need but open our eyes on the fair frame of things about us, and queftion our hearts how came they here: and our hearts would anfwer, *this hath God done*; *perceiving that it was his work.* The Atheift however hath difcovered the way of making a world, without calling to his affiftance the power and wifdom of God.

" Nullam rem e nihilo gigni divinitus unquam;"

is the principle, on which he proceeds to erect his fpecious building : how far it may be admitted, we will in the fequel examine.

I. If at the firft, or from eternity, NOTHING exifted; there never could have exifted any thing : fo far juft and
true

true is the poſition above aſſumed. SOMETHING therefore exiſted from all eternity.

That SOMETHING was either matter; or a ſubſtance different from matter. Inertion being an eſſential property of matter, mere matter could never have produced itſelf; for ſelf-exiſtence implies activity : it could not have produced itſelf even in a Chaotic, ſhapeleſs maſs. Something therefore muſt from eternity have exiſted, poſſeſt of active and higher powers, than matter poſſeſſes. That SOMETHING we ſtile God.

But admitting for a moment the former ſuppoſition, and conceiving of matter, as an eternal exiſtence ; from whence ſhall we ſuppoſe it to have derived thoſe beautiful and varying ſhapes, which we now behold ? On the moſt favourable ſuppoſition of its origin, a rude, indigeſted maſs ; from whence did it become poſſeſt of its power of diverſifying its motions and operations in

ſuch

such a manner, as to produce the wonderful variety of beings, that are found scattered upon the face of the earth?

SERMON II.

The atomists saw the defect of this scheme of Atheism: and therefore to self-existent matter they gave a power, which does not belong to it; they conferred motion on it, and introduced a million of self-existent, dancing atoms: a system of heathen philosophy, which, however blazoned with the ornaments of verse, is much of a piece with that of their theology; both highly poetic: and, notwithstanding the encomium, with which a modern historian of no small name hath distinguished the *pretty* theology of Julian,* both exceedingly absurd.

Necessary self-existence is the prime attribute of the Deity: something self-

* Gibbon's History of the Decline and Fall of the Roman Empire.

existent

existent is God. A million therefore of self-existing, self-moving atoms, are a million of Gods. And when those millions of atoms had danced themselves into shapeable existences, seas, rivers, mountains, trees, and the like: it was natural enough for the plastic powers of poetic imagination, to personify those eternal existences; who, according to the scheme of Epicurean philosophy, were Deities ready made to their hand: and hence, their Oreades, Naiades, &c. their Gods and Goddesses, of land, and of rivers, and even of the bowels of the earth.

But supposing for a moment the existence of motion, without admitting a mover: there is still wanting design. For a fortuitous dance of atoms is no more equal to the creation of a world, in which there are such marks of infinite wisdom, harmony, and design, as this of ours displays: than a fortuitous jumble of letters, to the composition of an
epic

epic poem; or of colours, to the delineation of a regular picture. For on the moſt advantageous idea of what matter is, and motion can do: that is no more than an inert, chaotic, maſs; and this a blind impulſe, eternally proceeding without deſtination.

To make one conceſſion further, and ſuppoſe, upon another ſyſtem of Atheiſm, matter to have eternally exiſted in the beautiful variety of ſhape and form, in which we now behold it; without ſome external ſupport, all thoſe beautiful appearances of things muſt long ago have ſunk into their original nothing. For matter, ſuch as the world is compoſed of, being in itſelf liable to corruption, animate ſubſtances, as well as inanimate, having all their riſe, their progreſs, and decay; their ſelf-exiſtence does not imply a greater degree of abſurdity, than their ſelf-ſupport from all eternity in the ſame form and ſtate.

From this view of the incompetence of matter, confidered in every light, to felf-exiftence and eternity, we muft admit fome fuperior principle; and acknowledge an eternal felf-exiftent caufe: fomething of power to create matter, which in itfelf poffeffes no active powers, confequently not the power of felf-exiftence: an exiftent caufe, poffeffing alfo wifdom and defign, equal to the diverfification obfervable in this fair frame of things about us. And that being is God.

To this beauty, order, and regularity, fo difcernible in the univerfe, the apoftle in my text particularly appeals; in proof of the exiftence and perfections of the Deity. And if this argument could be thought to want any corroborative; I might inftance the univerfal confent of mankind, in all ages of the world, and in every region: which concurrence of affent muft be a ftrong prefumption of truth.

For

For it contradicts every principle of reason, to imagine that by the constitution of human nature false principles should have been generally and uniformly infused into our minds; and that we should be naturally inclined to error: that, in this great truth of God's existence, the whole world should be taught to err; except the few, whose interest it may be, to wish the doctrine false, that they may live to the full enjoyment of their appetites and inclinations, without the molestation of conscience, and the alarms of fear. Nor can any other certain and general cause be assigned for so general an opinion, except the nature of the human mind: which hath this notion of a Deity born with it; and, as we may thence conclude, stamped upon it by the author of nature, the Deity himself. But I forbear to pursue this argument; or to dwell longer on this part of my subject: hastening to the second proposition; which was to reconcile the supersedure

SERMON of the general laws of nature, in the
II. cafe of miracles, with the wifdom and
goodnefs of that infinite being, who to
the operation of nature affigned thofe
laws.

II. To acknowledge a Deity, and yet
tie Him down by fuppofitions, which, if
pufhed to their utmoft length, would
leave Him with limited powers ; is to
throw over Atheifm fo thin a veil, as
hides nothing of it, but its name. This
however is the tendency of an argument
againft the reality of miracles, which
has been maintained with the greateft
confidence ; and is founded on the *impoffibility* of them, confiftent with the
attributes of the Deity. A miracle being a fuperfedure or alteration of the
eftablifhed courfe of nature, it is contended ; that if fuch alteration be for the
better, the courfe of nature was not
originally eftablifhed with infinite wifdom ; if for the worfe, it is an alteration
not confiftent with infinite goodnefs.

This

This argument, for it is a favourite one, hath been offered in another form, and with a happy change of words. " God," it is argued " cannot fuperfede " the courfe of things, he has eftablifh- " ed, without violating the laws of " nature." The word, *violate*, adds no new force to the argument: but it is aptly calculated to fling imputed cenfure on the oppofite opinion: as maintaining the reality of thofe extraordinary operations, at the expence of violating the facred laws of God and nature.

In form more full, and ftronger terms, I offer the argument; in the direct words of a celebrated effay, by zealous partizans ftill dealt out in detail, and held up in triumph. " A miracle is a " violation of the laws of nature: and " as a firm and unalterable experience " hath eftablifhed thefe laws, the proof " againft a miracle, from the very na- " ture of the fact, is as intire, as any

" argument

"argument from experience can be possibly imagined."*

The first part of the proposition, it is plain to observe, is an assertion without proof: unless the subsequent clause be intended to substantiate one, in the assumption, that *firm and unalterable experience hath established these laws.* But *firm and unalterable* experience constitutes such proof no longer, than till these laws are superseded; and then *firm and unalterable* experience proves in particular cases and for special purposes, a deviation from those general laws. And such deviation is as strongly established by *firm and unalterable experience*, as the former regularity itself. Nor can it, being God's immediate operation, or at least an act under his permission, with more propriety be stiled a violation of the laws of nature; than the mountainous waves of the sea, proudly overleap-

* See Hume's Essay on Miracles.

ing

ing the bounds which He had set them, deluging whole regions, and ingulphing cities,—or the dark spots, which astronomers observe increasingly to incrust the bright orb of the sun, in possible diminution both of its heat and light,—can be charged on his works, as violations of the general laws, He had assigned to their operation.

He, that had a power to direct nature according to certain general laws, must also have a power to control, and alter her movements. And such alteration, or control, is as much the act, either mediately or immediately, of infinite power and wisdom, as the general law itself. It is a part of that general law; which was formed with such a specific deviation. Whatever weight therefore may be ascribed to this argument; it in reality possesses none. It stands not in our way in proof, that such supersedure of the general laws of nature is impossible; as being incompatible either with infinite wisdom or power. The only question

SERMON II.

question then is, whether human testimony be sufficient to prove it: which will fall under an article of future discussion; being a point of enquiry, with which in the present case we are not concerned. Nothing more is in this state of the subject contended for; than that God can supersede the general laws of nature, without incurring the rash imputation of violating them.

But the author was led into this argument, by narrow notions of the divine agency. He has adverted to the Deity, as an artist; and to the structure of this world, as a complicated machine, of his framing; consisting of a variety of mechanic powers, which he puts into motion, assigning general movements to every distinct part; turns the piece of finished mechanism out of his hands, and leaves it in its various parts to pursue its destined operations: which it will invariably perform, unless some derangement of the parts impede and interrupt

terrupt its motions. Now were this representation of the Deity adequate and juft; the argument adduced muft be admitted of no inconfiderable weight. For as the great machine muft have come out of the hands of its Creator perfectly good, and was left without further attention to continue the courfe, He had prefcribed to it; every deviation from the order and courfe, He had fo prefcribed, would be a deterioration of his work.

But doth fuch an idea comport with the Creator of heaven and earth? And indeed what human idea will? Certainly however the idea of God, at firft creating and giving movements to the world, and then leaving it to purfue thofe motions no longer under his infpection, without his farther regard, without fupport:—fuch idea doth furely ill fuit the attributes of omnifcience and omniprefence. In his operations he knows neither beginning, middle, nor end.

With

With Him no diftance diftinguifhes time or place: He looks neither backwards nor forwards; the idea of FIRST, or LAST, notes not his actions: who is always, every where; and at one comprehenfive glance views every minute movement of every part of his innumerable works, in every period of their operations.

When at the firft, if, in application to God, we may properly ufe fuch a term as FIRST, He made the element of water yield to the impreffion of the human ftep; He made it alfo on a particular occafion to refift it: and the one particular occafional power was as much the given power of God, and as early given, as the other. And this given power to that part of nature, which performs it, is his law. With the fame almighty FIAT, which put the world in motion, He for a moment ftopped the movements of fome of its parts. At the fame moment, He faw them perform their accuftomed

tomed revolutions, and saw them halt: when, in scripture language, *the sun stood still on Gibeon, and the moon in the valley of Ajalon.* At the same instant, and with the same glance, he sees the sun travelling in his strength, and the moon's reflected beams enlivening the gloom of night; and also beholds, at the destined period of their dissolution, the one *turned into blood,* and the face of the *other darkened:* His hand alike directs both operations. Respecting Him, with whom time is not, when we speak of periods and of times; we should keep ever in mind, that we use those terms, because we know not how to express our ideas of Him more suitably. But thus far our ideas of God may attain: that acting always, as He demonstratively does, and present every where, as He necessarily is, when the operations of nature are most eccentric, equally as when most regular, they perform the divine will: and the unerring rectitude, with which He rules, or stops,

her

SERMON II. her motions, ever preserves the course, that nature may pursue, from the imputation of VIOLATION.

III. The point, which under the article of God's existence I proposed in the third and last place to consider, was the general principle of Materialism : as of tendency to degrade the divine nature. For when we magnify matter above its just claim and pretensions, and ascribe to it perfections, which it doth not possess; when we attribute to it perception, memory, reflection, those intellectual faculties, a ray of divinity, if indeed the image of God be in any degree stamped upon us: we must take care we be not led step by step, at last to degrade the divine nature, and materialise even the Deity himself.

That such dangerous tendency in the principles of materialism is not matter of vain presumption, but of fact; the direct acknowledgment of one of the most

most determined materialists of this age evinces; who observes, that "the doctrine of the materiality of man has been charged with leading to Atheism."* And then in the very same work, while he affects to remove, he proceeds to establish, the charge: employing two sections to prove, that "the nature of the Deity is material." The antient philosophy of Epicurus conferred motion on self-existent matter: the modern materialist, more bountiful, endows it with perceptive and intellectual powers. If that were Atheism; I fear this will rank little lower. Such principles, if they lead men to conceive of God, not as he is, but *turn the glory of God into a corruptible nature*, are equally derogatory from the sublime nature of the Deity, as direct Atheism itself. And the author's candid acknowledgment of the existence of such a charge is, on the subject we are now investigating, sufficient to justify

* Priestley's Disquisitions on Matter and Spirit.

my endeavours to guard againſt principles of ſo deſperate tendency.

The chain of reaſoning, on which the Materialiſt proceeds, ſuppoſes, that to enable one being to act upon another, they muſt each poſſeſs ſome common property: the mind therefore, if qualified to act upon the body, muſt have ſome common property of matter; and for the ſame reaſon ſo muſt the Deity himſelf. But what has the properties of matter, is matter. This is in brief the argument in ſupport of the doctrine of materialiſm: and ſuch is the deſperate length, to which it goes.

Let us examine this train of reaſoning, and argue on the fact in the extreme: let us ſuppoſe the truth of the concluſion, that the Deity poſſeſſes ſome property common to matter; and aſk what known property it is. Not inertion, moſt aſſuredly: for every attribute of the Deity implies activity. Not ſolidity:

dity: for in Him, whether the Chriſtian's God, or the heathen philoſopher's *anima mundi, we live, and move, and have our being.* Not ſhape: for that has bounds. In ſhort, not any property of matter, that can be aſcertained. Every power of the mind, and every property obſervable in matter, are ſo eſſentially different; that the idea of homogeneity in the two ſubſtances is too extravagant to be admitted on any other ground, than a direct proof of the impoſſibility of the action of ſpirit on matter, without the exiſtence of ſome common property. Our incapacity to comprehend in what manner ſuch action, ſo circumſtanced, can be exerted, is not ſufficient, againſt every appearance that it is ſo, to deſtroy the poſſibility of the fact.

Yet however bold the aſſertion is, that ſpirit *cannot* act upon matter without poſſeſſing ſome common property of it; and however falſe it may be: it muſt with proper diffidence be acknowledged, ed, that it is difficult to conceive how thought can come into immediate contact with a fubftance fo apparently oppofite to it, as matter. But humbly confidering how little we know of the laws, by which God governs the world; though ignorant of the caufe, may we not, inftructed by the effect, fuppofe fome fecret law of nature exifting, fome fine link between the two fubftances, by which the mind may receive its fenfations and ideas; and through which it may exercife its operations, excite motions, and perform actions? We know, in the chain of material beings how nice the links of nature; we know, how nearly the quadruped approaches the feathered tribe; how nearly the inhabitant of the watery element him, that grazes on the plain; the vegetative the animal being. And I conceive it not improbable, much lefs impoffible, which is fufficient to urge againft a direct impoffibility; that there may be fome fine link between the material and the immaterial world,

fome

some medium of action, which, if known, would satisfy the doubts of philosophic arrogance.

My design in this discourse has been, to establish the proof of God's existence, as the foundation of all religion: and with all humility so far to investigate the Divine nature, as forming an object of religious worship; of that pure form of worship especially, the truth of which in the sequel of these discourses I shall proceed to evince. And if the reflections on this subject, which I have now offered, have any weight; they will conduce to mould our minds to the study of ourselves. And when, convinced of our own weakness and imperfection, we raise our thoughts to the contemplation of the Deity; we shall, from what we are, from what we feel within, and behold without us, derive irrefragable and increasing proofs of his existence. We shall learn to think humbly of ourselves, and exaltedly of that infinitely perfect and adorable Being, who called us from nothing; and gave us all that we at prefent enjoy, or in reverfion hope for. And when the enlarged mind expatiates on his power; we fhall tremble at the idea of fixing any thing like a limit to it: when we endeavour to fearch into the infcrutable treafures of his wifdom; we fhall exert every fertile power of imagination, to admire and revere it: and when we prefume to employ our thoughts on his nature; we fhall feparate from it every idea, that fuits not with the higheft excellence we can attribute to the moft fublime and exalted Being: and after all this ftretch of heart, and foul, and ftrength, to think worthily of Him, we fhall have to lament the weaknefs of our conception, and the imperfection of our ideas; fatisfied that, high as the enraptured mind can raife them, they fall beneath, infinitely beneath, the elevated fubject, on which they are employed.

SERMON III.

Job, xxxi. 4.

Doth He not fee my ways, and count all my fteps?

FROM the evidence of God's exiſtence, which was the ſubject of my laſt diſcourſe; we will now proceed to the proofs, we have of his providence. It has been ſhewn, that the world is the production of a Being infinite in wiſdom and power, whom we ſtile God: the point of doctrine next to be proved is, that this World, this whole ſyſtem of created things, is ſuper-intended, governed, and directed by that Almighty God, who made it. And indeed there is ſuch

SERMON III.

such a natural and necessary connection between the belief of God's existence, and superintendence; that he, who believes the one, would he think consistently, must believe the other likewise. If we believe there is a God, who made the world; we must likewise believe that the same God, who made the world, doth govern it too. For matter is as incompetent to support it's own existence, as to create itself; nor is chance better qualified to govern a world, than to make one: and we have already seen, how unapt matter is for the active office of creation; and how unequal chance is to the formation of a world, which displays such harmony, regularity, and consistence. But from appearances let us proceed to proofs.

The power of God, displayed in the government of the world, may be considered in a double view:

First,

First, in respect to the material world; in which He is acknowledged as ordering, and directing the changes and revolutions of nature : His will, and governing power, being the universal law, which it observes.

And secondly we may consider the superintendence of God, as displayed in a moral and religious view; in His dispensations and government, respecting the rational world : including the general state, œconomy, and conduct of mankind. And under this head I propose a further enquiry into the reality of a particular, as well as general, providence : addressed to the consideration of those, who, under the affectation of enlarged ideas of the Divine nature, pretend to suppose it an opinion unworthy of Him, to ascribe to his immediate interposition occurrences, which are sometimes stiled providential ; but which, though apparently extraordinary, fall within the common course prescribed to nature,

however

however hidden from us, and secret may be the immediate causes of them.

I. First, then, the general notion of providence is God's care of all the creatures He has made; which must consist in preserving and upholding their beings and natures, and in such acts of government, as the good order of the world, the arrangement of things, their secret dependencies, and correspondent effects require. And that there is such a manifest general ordination and adaptation of things in the natural world, that they exactly suit the purposes of each other, and contribute mutually to the universal good of the great whole; that the common necessities of mankind are graciously provided for, and supplied in the usual course of things, and according to the general laws of nature, which infinite wisdom and goodness originally established; that the heavenly bodies are constituted, and their movements directed, with exact proportion to one another in

their

OF THE CHRISTIAN RELIGION. 59

their feveral ftations and circuits; are SERMON
truths, that have with fuitable expref- III.
fions of admiration been obferved and acknowledged by thofe, who have pene-
trated fartheft into ftudies and enquiries
of that kind.

When we proceed to a more particular inveftigation of this interefting doctrine of a divine providence, the mind
is ftruck with the obferved fubfiftence
of things in the fame ftructure; and
with the fame progreffion, through the
feveral ages of their being. In this confideration is involved a two-fold circumftance; their ftability, and their arrangement: the one inconceivable without
active intelligence, and the other without fupport.

Though neither matter, nor motion,
nor both united, have been found in
themfelves competent to the creation of
the world: there can be no doubt, but,
under the direction of the Divine archi-
tect,

tect, they conftitute the compofition of the vifible univerfe. It was not therefore wonderful, that fome philofophers fhould have conferred on them the principle of felf-exiftence: and it was confiftent with fuch opinion, to attribute to them the powers of confervation and fupport. But from the idea of matter, attenuate and modify it as you will, inactivity, it has been already obferved, is infeparable. If therefore effentially paffive, and confequently not felf-exiftent, but created; impotent to produce, it muft be equally impotent to preferve itfelf. For in reality how doth production differ from prefervation, except as an act exerted from its continuance? One moment of active being implies, in an inert mafs, as confiderable a difficulty as another. It requires the fame power to confirm a fecond moment of action, as to affign a firft; a third, as a fecond: and fo on through all the parts of duration. And if fo, from the fame principle muft be derived the continuance of of the world's exiftence, as the origin of it.

SERMON III.

In the fame manner with regard to motion; we cannot conceive of it, without admitting a caufe. From a blind and fenfelefs caufe can proceed only a blind and indefinite effect: that is, in the prefent inftance a tendency every way; which is plainly equivalent to a tendency no way, or to reft. A tendency, in any given or definite way, denotes felection and direction; and thefe again, immediately or ultimately, an external intelligent mover. How then can that, which could neither begin, nor guide, continue itfelf? There is befides in every impulfe a diminution of motion: fo that whatever momentum is communicated to the body impelled, re-action is known to take from the impellent. What then can repair this continual lofs; or, in other words, fupport a conftant motion, like the revolutions of the globe in one regular tenor; except an inceffant

SERMON
III.
ceffant action: which brings us at once to the inceffant intervention of a superintending Deity?

Let us next advert to the additional circumftance of arrangement. Survey, and it is a delightful entertainment to furvey, the productions and provifions of nature: you will perceive on the firft obfervation variety, curiofity, co-operation, and mutual fubfervience; fucceffions without failure, greatnefs without difproportion, complication without confufion. Obferve particularly the nice difpofition of the univerfe, of which this orb of ours forms a part; the diftribution of the larger planets in wider and remoter orbits, that their gravity may not interfere with the fafety or velocity of the fmaller; the meafured diftance of the earth from the fun, whofe approach or recedure with any fenfible variation might endanger its being, or all its comforts.

Then

OF THE CHRISTIAN RELIGION. 63

Then let us bring our reflections Sermon
nearer home; and observe this globe of III.
earth that we inhabit, and its productions. What an elegant and beneficial
assemblage do we behold springing from
mere mould, a cold, lumpish, crumbling
substance; not grateful to any sense, nor
possessed in appearance of any prolific
virtue! With what exquisite art, accommodating structure to character and exertion, are particular creatures organised;
severally destined to form and fill up a
compact, regular, and complete system:
a system, the composition of which consisting of materials infinitely numerous,
infinitely diversified, hath stood for near
six thousand years one and the same;
uninjured in its form, unimpaired in its
parts, unobstructed in its movements!
Consider this complex wonder; and who
can hesitate to conclude, that every thing
is sustained, guided, and uniformly rein-
stated, by a vigilant providence, " great
in council, and mighty in work."

For

SERMON III.

For in short wherever there is an effect, it must have a cause answerable; a determinate effect, a determining cause; a perpetual or periodical effect, a permanent one. Thus order implies design, symmetry contrivance, beauty workmanship, regularity guidance, unerring regularity wisdom, limitation influence, utility forecast. And all these, existing in infinite circumstances, declare an infinite mind, operating in the appointment of them with infinite discernment, and in the preservation of them with infinite attention; which is in other words, a presiding providence. On this subject engaged, one cannot help giving scope to imagination, and reflecting on the infinite pleasure it will give the enlarged mind, when admitted to a nearer view of things, than our converse in this world admits, to explore the curiosities and exhaustless wonders of nature: to view, with what art and contrivance each particular creature is made; and how the several parts of this

great

great machine are fitted to each other, and continue on from generation to generation a regular and uniform world. Mutually connected and dependent, each is fitted to the ufes and purpofes of their feveral natures, all ferviceable and affiftant to one another, and every individual neceffary to the whole.

On fuch a furvey, to matter and motion, to every caufe a fertile imagination can fuggeft, analogy will force us to add defign. For by a fortuitous concourfe of things we fee nothing regular effected in works of art: by what rule of reafoning then are we to expect it in the operations of nature? And with defign, we muft admit of a defigner: that is, a Being of wifdom, to plan; and of power, the extent of which we meafure by the execution of the plan. In nature's works confider the defign, and examine the execution of it; and impute them, who can, to lefs than infinite wifdom and power. Such were the reflections, which, Claudian tells us, cured his doubts

SERMON III. doubts refpecting a fuperintending providence: the defcription is elegant, and the reafoning juft; with that defcription, the elegance of the paffage, and the propriety of fentiment it conveys, will I truft plead my excufe for concluding the argument drawn from obfervations on the material world.

"Sæpe * mihi dubiam traxit fententia mentem,
"Curarent fuperi terras, an nullus ineffet
"Rector, & incerto fluerent mortalia cafu.
"Aft cum difpofiti quæfiffem fœdera mundi,
"Præfcriptofque mari fines, annifque meatus,
"Et lucis noctifque vices; tunc omnia rebar
"Confilio firmata Dei, qui lege moveri
"Sidera, qui fruges diverfo tempore nafci,
"Qui variam Phœben alieno jufferit igne
"Compleri, Solemque fuo; porrexerit undis
"Littora; tellurem medio libraverit axe."
CLAUD. in Ruf. lib. iii.

II. I proceed 2dly to confider the fuperintendence of God as difplayed in a moral

* Oft have I doubted, whether power divine
Direct this world with wifdom and defign;
Or

moral and religious view, in his difpenfa- SERMON
tions and government, refpecting the rati- III.
onal world; including the general ftate,
œconomy, and conduct of mankind.

And in this difcuffion the firft great
argument, that offers, is the general ad-
miniftration of the world in favour of
virtue. Vice is not always punifhed
here, nor virtue always rewarded; nor
indeed ought it to be fo: for then this
world would be a ftate of rewards and
punifhments; and not, as it is, a ftate

> Or all things rife, decay, recede, advance,
> Caufe and effect the random work of chance.
> But when the frame of nature meets my mind,
> It's various links harmonioufly combined;
> The bounds, that check the ocean's wild career,
> The deftined periods of the meafured year;
> The brightly-beaming day, the fcowling night,
> Succeeding darknefs, and returning light:
> My doubts are banifh'd, 'gainft each vain furmife,
> GOD ftands reveal'd, all-mighty, and all-wife.
> By Him the bounties of the earth are given,
> He framed the laws, that rule the orbs of heaven:
> He bade the ocean, keep its channell'd place,
> He hung the well-poifed world in empty fpace.

of trial and probation: and thus would one of the cleareſt and ſtrongeſt arguments in proof of a future ſtate be taken away. But though there be wiſe reaſons, why ſome virtuous men ſhould be unhappy in this life, and ſome vicious men proſperous; for this world not being a place of judgment, but a ſtate of preparation, divine juſtice does not require, that every good or bad man ſhould, according to his works, be reſpectively recompenſed here: yet the wiſdom, and goodneſs, and juſtice of God do require, that in general virtue ſhould be rewarded, and ſin puniſhed; and that in ſuch degrees, and in ſuch a manner, as ſhall lay all reaſonable reſtraints on the luſts and paſſions of men, and proportionably promote and encourage the exertion of their virtues. How far the face of things about us tends to confirm this opinion, let us next inquire; contenting ourſelves, where demonſtration cannot be had, with the higheſt degree of probability.

It

It is impossible to parcel out by weight or admeasurement the quantity of good and evil, that falls out in this life to refpective individuals; fo as demonftratively to afcertain the fact, that even in this world there is a confiderable preponderation of happinefs in favour of virtue: but as the truth of this opinion forms a very powerful argument, in proof of a wife and good prefiding power; I fubmit the following reflections in fupport of it. When we obferve mankind in general, the wicked as well as the religious, *him that feareth God, and him that feareth Him not*, fo anxious as they appear to be, that their children fhould purfue virtuous courfes; we muft conclude fuch a general defire to have as general a motive: which is their happinefs and profperity in life. And though this motive, which to the temporalift is a leading one, be to the good and virtuous only fecondary: its effect is in both inftances the fame; forming an argument from univerfal confent, that according

SERMON
III.

ing to the present dispensations of providence, or, if this mode of expression appear an assumption of the point in doubt, according to the present course of things, success even in this world is the consequence of a virtuous conduct.

In proof of this truth, permit me to refer the argument, in another shape, to the discrimination of every man's own judgment. Let us revolve in our minds a certain number of our friends and acquaintances, whom we know to be men of virtue; and an equal number, whom we know, or have great reason to believe, to be vicious characters: then let us reflect, whether the virtuous or vicious characters appear to enjoy the most happiness in themselves and their connections; and from such reflection concurrent opinion, I am persuaded, will confirm the truth of the assertion " that " happiness, in the ordinary and gene- " ral course of things, is even in this " life the handmaid and attendant on " virtue."

" virtue." And such general dispensation of things, in favour of virtue, is a demonstration of a super-intending providence, equally and infinitely wise and good.

There was a sect of ancient philosophers, who carried this opinion so far; that, to obviate the argument against a wise and good presiding power, deduced from the permission and sufferance of evil, as happening indiscriminately to all men, they denied the reality of it. This caused them to adopt some extraordinary tenets, which led to wild and whimsical inferences. But both the tenets and inferences were less pernicious, and much nearer to truth, than those opposite doctrines; that, to exculpate providence from the apparent irregularities and inequalities in moral dispensations, excluded Him from having any concern in the government of the world: referring it to the management of an imaginary principle, which they stiled

SERMON III.

ſtiled chance, and thought better calculated to preſide in ſuch a mixt and inexplicable ſtate of things. For though it muſt be acknowledged, that there are evils in life, and that they occaſionally happen to the virtuous, as well as the wicked: yet would it on nice examination be found, that thoſe evils are leſs in degree, and in number fewer, than is generally ſuppoſed; and more frequently the conſequences of human imprudence, than the querulous diſpoſition of human nature will readily admit.

Scarcely indeed is there a more common ſubject of declamation and complaint, than the inequality obſervable in the temporal diſpenſations of providence. But giving ſomething to ſelf-love, which in our own eyes is apt to magnify our deſervings above their real value; ſomething to diſappointment, which often ſits heavier on our minds, than reaſon will juſtify; and ſomething to that depravity of heart, which inclines us to

make

OF THE CHRISTIAN RELIGION. 73

make a falſe eſtimate of our own happi- Sermon
neſs, from compariſon with the apparent III.
happineſs and proſperity of others ; we
muſt acknowledge, there is a preponderation of happineſs in this world, ſufficient to prove the government of a wiſe
and good providence : involving at the
ſame time ſuch a mixture of evil, in the
various courſe of events, as clearly in-
ſtructs us to look beyond this ſcene of
things for an exact adjuſtment of rewards
and puniſhments

In ſhort from a fair and candid view
of things about us, however diſcontent
may magnify preſent diſſatisfactions, in-
tricacies into irregularities, trials into
hardſhips, impunity into proſperity ; it
appears inconceivable, without admitting a ſecret reſtraint on actions or their
effects by the immediate interpoſition of
a Divine providence, but that the good
would be far greater ſufferers, than they
are ; and that ſociety, if not diſſolved,
would be far more deranged and diſ-
quieted,

SERMON III.

quieted, than we experience it : confidering the prevalence of corruption, the eagerneſs of rapine, the turbulence of ambition, the unrulineſs of paſſion, and the malignity of diſappointment.

From the confideration of a general, let us next extend our enquiries to the doctrine of a particular, providence : in the admiſſion of which the chief difficulty ſeems to lie in a narrow mode of conceiving of God, and inadequate terms of expreſſion. We are apt to confider the care and management of the world, agreeably to our ideas of care and management, as a laborious operation : and the mode of expreſſion, we uſe, contributes to inculcate ſuch ideas. We ſpeak of God's taking charge of the affairs of the world, of His adminiſtration of them, of His adjuſtment of cauſes and effects, and the like : terms, which we are forced to employ, for want of ſuch as would better ſuit that infinite and incomprehenſible mind ; which at once

glances

OF THE CHRISTIAN RELIGION. 75

glances through time and nature, and with omnipotence of will directs, governs, and controls.

Such opinion of the government of the univerfe, as a work of pains and labour, was I conceive an argument of additional weight to that already fuggefted; in inducing the Epicureans, a fect of philofophers confiderable both for their learning and numbers, to imagine the government of the univerfe too troublefome, to engage the attention of the Deity. They confidered Him, as by nature neceffarily and perfectly happy, and therefore above invefting himfelf with a charge; which to conduct with uniform and confiftent regularity, they fuppofed, muft occafion care and confideration, and of courfe detract from His felicity. The idea is elegantly defcribed by the Latin poet; himfelf a zealous advocate for the doctrine, and the fect.

* Omnis

SERMON III.

Omnis * enim per se divûm natura necesse † 'st
Immortali ævo summâ cum pace fruatur,
Semota ab nostris rebus, sejunctaque longe;
Nam privata dolore omni, privata periclis,
Ipsa suis pollens opibus, nihil indiga nostri,
Nec bene promeritis capitur, nec tangitur Ira.
                                LUCRETIUS, lib. 1.

On this opinion, I have only to observe a narrowness of mind; which could suppose the direction and management of so small a part of the unbounded works of creation, a care and trouble to its omnipotent Creator. Far be it however from man's presumption, to affect to

---

* The gods by fate and nature must enjoy
Immortal life, and bliss without alloy;
Sequester'd far from earth, and earthly things,
The threats of danger, and of pain the stings:
In the perfection of their own high powers
Supremely happy, they require not ours;
Our actions all indifferently regard,
Hold up no scourge, and tender no reward.

† The word *necesse*, in this passage, seems to allude to FATE: a necessarian principle, which in the Epicurean system, controls even the gods themselves.

point out in what manner, He directs and governs His innumerable works; of which this univerfe of ours is but a point: certainly not by toil and labour; nor by any means detracting from fupreme felicity. He governs; as He created: and the fublime * defcription, given by Mofes, of His creation of the world, will perhaps beft fuit his government of it too; effected by the influence of an energetic volition, unimpeded by difficulties, unincumbered by diftraction.

To fuppofe every diftribution of good and evil, of happinefs and mifery, by certain general laws to have been irreverfibly ordained to take place in this life, when nature was firft put in motion, is in effect to limit the operations of Him, who impofed thofe laws on na-

* The paffage alluded to is noticed by Longinus, as an uncommon inftance of the true fublime.

ture;

ture; and by such restrictions in a degree to exclude Him from His own works: it is taking from Him every other, than a sustaining power. Whereas by referring such general succession of events to a concatenation of causes decreed at the formation of all things, the wisdom and goodness of God in particular instances, and as occasions present themselves, applying the established laws of nature to the benefit, comfort, and correction of individuals; we learn to reconcile the particular dispensations of providence with the general course of nature. Thus we know, certain causes will produce certain effects: yet we see in the moral world varying effects often derived from an apparent similarity of causes. Infinite wisdom sees what effects in particular circumstances, and for particular, and wise, and good reasons ought to follow; and those He directs to follow: and on this ground is founded the poet's reflection, which has been abused to false

and

and pernicious inferences, that "whatever is, is right." That is, whatever event takes place, it is the refult of certain fecret caufes; wifely modified and directed by the Almighty Governor of the world, fo as to be the beft refult that could happen from the caufes that produced it.

Our eyes difcover to us nothing, and from reflection we know little, of the fecret fprings, by which the occurrences of this life are moved. In afferting the particular difpenfations of providence; we do not preclude their afpect to other objects and effects, than the fimple one we particularly note. On the contrary, we may with good reafon conclude, that all the difpenfations of providence are fo conducted, as to have a further influence; than in any particular inftance, and on the fingle individual, to which they may appear to us to be principally directed. We may fuppofe each, like a link in the vaft chain of nature's moral courfe,

to

to have respect to the great whole. For who can say, that the Author of nature cannot so manage both the natural, and moral course of things; as to make the blessings and corrections, He shall will to individuals, harmonise with His general laws. And if no good reason can be produced in proof that He cannot do it, that is, if such act imply no contradiction; we may justly conclude He does it: because such operation enlarges our ideas of His power, wisdom, and goodness; of which the utmost reach of imagination will not enable us to think sufficiently high. Every day's experience informs us of escapes from dangers, deliverances from distress, the detection of secret sins so unexpected, so unassignable to any known cause, that we attribute them to the immediate interposition and interference of God: who must see and observe them, because He is always every where; and whose energetic power, unsustained by which the course of nature would fail, what He sees

sees and observes, must direct and govern too.

When men speak of the general laws of nature; they can only understand those general causes and effects, with which they are acquainted. Those, we are not to suppose, God will upon every light occasion suspend, or alter. But are there not, may there not be, hidden causes, which we cannot see; by which providence acts in his particular dispensations? Such in the moral world there must be. For the progress and direction of the passions are in different men combined with such a variety of adventitious circumstances; as seem to require from providence different degrees of encouragement, assistance, and correction: such different degrees, as cannot depend upon any general system, or course of things predetermined by God ; and therefore infer the necessity of particular dispensations. And the moral course of things, so disposed and attempered, produces

duces that general harmony, which is experienced, and eafily reconciled, by the admiffion of an interfering and interpofing providence; every where and always prefent as He is, noting all things as He does, and univerfally energetic as our beft conceptions of His nature reprefent Him.

In fhort to difcard the belief of a parcicular providence, is the next ftep to throwing afide the belief of any providence whatever: for it muft be almoft immaterial to individuals, whether there be any providence, or not; if every thing be governed by predetermined laws. On fuch a fuppofition, where is the affiftance, to which patient merit may apply? If one uniform tenor, without refpect to particular perfons, and particular cafes, prevail in the operations of nature; diftrefs has no where to look for comfort, the workings of the pious heart in prayer are inefficacious and vain.

Hence

Hence then it appears, that the denial of such a power to providence, in itself the height of presumption, leads to the lowest depths of desperation. For how must it mortify a thinking mind, for a moment to imagine; that the Almighty, after having created the universe, and ordained laws for its general government, satisfied with having furnished it with inhabitants, and provided for their common support, sent them to succeed each other on this great stage; exposed to innumerable evils, which it is not in their power to shun; and deprived of the protection of that Being, who alone is able to shield us from them, or, what is more desireable, to convert them to our advantage. At that moment we cease to be encouraged with the lively hopes, that in our endeavours, if we deserve the Divine assistance, we shall enjoy it; in our dangers, if we merit deliverance, it will be providentially vouchsafed us; in distress, if virtue arm us, God will make the angry shaft of adversity, " Telum " imbelle

SERMON III.

" imbelle fine ictu," fall harmlefs at our feet.

What hath been offered, eftablifhing, as I have endeavoured to do, the doctrine of a Providence, particular as well as general, inculcates by practical confequence the Chriftian fortitude of truft. If the world be of God's creation, what He created with power, He muft govern with exactnefs: and therefore we may reft affured, there muft be a meaning in the permiffion, a propriety in the tendency of every event. On this perfuafion let us repofe with fubmiffive and patient truft, that whatever incidents of affliction or furprife occur; they are founded in defign, and their end is expedient. An unerring fuper-intendant ordains, an all-pervading eye obferves, and omni-prefent power directs them. To that adorable power let us look up; affured, that though in this mixt ftate of things evil be unavoidable, that evil, God can and does attemper with appendages

dages of good, fupplied by fecret means; thofe means conducted, with infinite wifdom and defign, with every poffible attention to the deferving.

SERMON IV

Pſalm xcv. 6.

O come let us worſhip and bow down; let us kneel before the Lord our Maker : for He is our God, and we are the people of his paſture.

SERMON IV.

IN evidence, that the world was originally made by a Being infinite in wiſdom and power; and that a power, no leſs perfect than that which made the world, directs, governs and upholds it in that harmony and regularity, which is ſo conſpicuous through the whole range of created beings ; the arguments adduced have, I truſt, been found to approach very near to demonſtration : as a truth deducible from theſe doctrines,
my

my next subject of enquiry is the obligation of religious worship.

SERMON IV.

And in this investigation my design is first to consider at large the general proposition.

Secondly, to examine the principle, that lifts up the pious heart to Heaven in prayer.

And in the third and last place to evince the close connection, that God Almighty hath ordained between religion and the social duties: so close, that without the former, civil society could not subsist.

I. First, then as to the general obligation of religion. A capacity to discover that there is a God, who made and preserves us: and that we are not able to do the one or the other of ourselves, indispensably requires us to love, honour, and serve that Maker and Preserver in every instance

and

SERMON IV. and action of our lives. For as long as we regard exiftence as a bleffing; fo long do we acknowledge ourfelves indebted to the giver and preferver of life. Now as we are able to infer an obligation for a benefit received; fuch fufficiency of knowledge in us, in regard to the benefits, we have from our great Creator received, is of itfelf a true and proper foundation for religious worfhip: and every creature capable of making fuch an inference, as every reafonable creature is, becomes therefore fubjected to the duty of gratitude; and from a confcious fenfe of gratitude to God flow the duties of religion. Thus conclufive is natural reafon, in proving the neceffity of religious worfhip among all beings, who poffefs a degree of intelligence equal to that of man.

And experience confirms that in fact, the propriety of which reafon evidences to us in theory. For among all nations, be their notions more or lefs refined, religious

ligious worſhip prevails. The moſt bar- Sermon IV.
barous and uncivilifed nations, as well
antient as modern, if their ſtate be
thoroughly enquired into, we ſhall find
had a religion, though ſometimes a very
depraved one; and offered up prayers,
and made adorations, though the object
of them has been a ſerpent, or a calf.
Even the wretched barbarians, in the
South Seas, whom the late diſcoveries
of modern travellers have made known
to us, though ſome of them almoſt
without clothes, or houſes, were none
of them obſerved to be without their
God.

From a practice ſo univerſal it appears, that God has ſtamped an image of Himſelf on the human mind ſo deeply, that the greateſt corruption of mankind has not been able entirely to erafe it; that He has naturally inculcated the method of acknowledging Him the ſupreme cauſe of all things by prayer and adoration ſo ſtrongly, as the loweſt depravation

Sermon IV.

tion of manners cannot abfolutely abolifh. And hence we may infer, that religion is a reafonable fervice, and a duty abfolutely required of us: or why did God, who made us, and never acts in vain, imprint fuch a notion on the human mind; if it be a matter of no confequence, and calculated for no ufe. But is it a matter of no confequence, to offer up our tribute of praife to that great fountain of goodnefs, from whom all our bleffings flow? Is it a matter of no confequence, to afcribe to Him the honour due unto His name: to pay juft homage to Almighty God, the Lord of Lords, and King of Kings? Or, is it not rather natural to conceive, that the infinitely great Creator of all things, when in fuch manifeftation of His adorable perfections He defigned the general happinefs, alfo involved in it a difplay of his own glory: willing that they fhould be acknowledged and reverenced, loved and praifed by intelligent creatures? And fuch acknowledgment accordingly

becomes

becomes a natural duty, and has the first moral claim to univerſal obſervance. For as honour in general is the homage paid to conſpicuous excellencies, and eſpecially to beneficent virtues : ſo religion, which is the higheſt honour, is appropriately due to God ; the moſt abſolute Being in all perfections, and our ſovereign Benefactor.

Our homage can not indeed add to the greatneſs of the Almighty : it can contribute nothing to His glory. He alſo knows our neceſſities without our information ; He knows what we have need of, before we aſk ; and how to impart to us good things, better than we to aſk them : ſo great are our ideas of the majeſty of an all-wiſe Almighty God. Yet to refuſe that homage, would be a ſinful omiſſion in us : as it is a conſtant acknowledgment of the exiſtence of a God, a continual memorial to us of our own littleneſs and dependence, and of His tranſcendent greatneſs and
ſuperintending

superintending providence. We offer praifes and thankfgiving to God for His mercies daily and hourly reached out to us; not that He can receive any additional honour from the praifes, that duft and afhes can beftow; but to make fuch difplay of His honour and glory, as rational creatures are enabled to proclaim; to teftify a grateful fenfe of His mercies reached out to us, and our own inability to render more: as a proof that we feel thofe mercies, and exercife the faculties, He hath conferred on us, in a becoming manner, and according to their proper ufe. We implore His protection in dangers, His deliverance out of afflictions, and His fupport againft the force of temptations, not that we fuppofe Him ignorant of our weakneffes or our wants: but in pious atteftation of our entire dependence on Him for every evil we avoid, and for every good we in this life enjoy; as a pledge of our belief in His omnipotence, of our reliance on His mercies, our refignation to the difpenfations of

OF THE CHRISTIAN RELIGION. 93

of His providence: and in teftimony of a full affurance of His provident concern for His whole creation.

SERMON IV.

Thus general is the fenfe of religion: and fo univerfal the obfervance of it. And thus clearly doth it prefs on us, as an indifpenfable duty. The object of religious worfhip, it is acknowledged, is not always the fame; nor even the principle of it: fome worfhip the fun, and fome a crocodile; fome a good being, and fome a bad one; fome through love, and fome through fear. Yet fuch variety proves nothing againft the general truth of religion, and the confequent obligation to obferve it. On the contrary, like counterfeit coins, it tends to prove one of real value; of value to be counterfeited. And if there be one religion, which fhines with more extraordinary characters of truth, than the reft; it forms a fubject, of every thing on this fide the grave moft worthy of ferious inveftigation :

SERMON IV.

vestigation: for without religion we are not men.

Reason indeed is generally supposed to be the distinguishing mark or characteristic of human nature: but perhaps religion is a much better. Reason, brutes have in common with mankind, and some brutes a considerable degree of it: or at least they possess something so much like reason, that it is difficult to draw the line of distinction between them. But no traits of religion do we discover in any of them. Religion, the knowledge and service of God, is the prerogative of man: it is the most reasonable and honourable employment, of which human nature is capable: it leads to an intercourse with God himself; which, while mankind acknowledge a God supreme, if they would acknowledge Him to any good purpose, the voice of reason and the impulse of nature, excite them to cultivate by acts of adoration and prayer.

II. This

OF THE CHRISTIAN RELIGION. 95

II. This fubject of prayer hath exer- SERMON
cifed the pens both of poets and philo- IV.
fophers in the the heathen world. And
amongft the infpired writers the prince
and poet of Ifrael is moft frequent in
his exhortations to it : and his expreffions
always mark the fervour of an interefted
heart. " O Thou, that heareft prayer,
' fays he'; to thee fhall all flefh come."
It is indeed a duty fo univerfal ; that all
mankind with an unforced affent agree in
the obfervance of it. Let us then, as
was propofed in the fecond place, with
fome minutenefs enter into the principle
of a duty, that in every age and country
hath obtained fo univerfal obfervance.

In the common intercourfe of life between man and man, between fuperiours
and inferiours, it will often happen that
favours are conferred; which thofe, on
whom they are conferred, have not
ability to repay. Yet fome return the
common principles of juftice require,
and prompt the perfon who receives
them

Sermon IV.

them to make. What return then shall extreme impotence render; and the benefactor's knowledge of that impotence demand? What, but the tribute of a grateful mind. The same reasoning will apply to the Deity; only in an infinitely higher degree: as infinitely higher, as the blessings of creation and preservation are above those accidental enjoyments, that depend on them. And such affection of the mind, as mankind feels for those inestimable blessings, naturally produces that glow of gratitude; which the enraptured heart pours out in the effusions of pious praise. Hence is deducible the duty of prayer: which resting on the doctrine of a particular providence, that doctrine in my last discourse I particularly applied myself to establish: intending, under the present article of enquiry, a more particular discussion of the duty resulting from it.

Man feels a thousand wants, which he cannot of himself supply; he foresees dangers,

dangers, which he knows not how to shun; he finds himself involved in difficulties, from which he perceives all human art and power incompetent to relieve him. In this emergency, nature, that in indelible characters hath graven the existence of God on the human heart, teaches him likewise the use of that innate knowledge, by secret admonitions to invoke his Creator's aid. If the former notion be natural to the human mind, and what is universal must be so; the latter, which is only the application of the former, must be so too. Those prayers, suggested by the impulse of nature in short ejaculations, the exercise of reason afterward matured into form, with length and expressive solemnity: and, from the use of private votaries, they became extended to public assemblies. And such public celebration of divine worship, more or less simple, as the respective people are more or less civilised, or rude, hath extended as far as the empire of reason prevails.

G Now

SERMON IV.

Now this duty of prayer, so natural to the human mind, and by communities so universally practised, is supported on the reality of a particular providence. For if at the time, the world was made, the laws of nature were given; general, invariable laws, which nature was bound to pursue; the Deity enthroned in majesty sublime, aloof as it were from his own works, or at most an unactive spectator of them, never interposing his power through second causes, to divert evil, to inflict correction, to save and to destroy; on what ground should we address the throne of heaven, for protection in time of danger, for support amidst temptations, or in times of distress for deliverance out of trouble: subjects, which, while we live in the world, must form a part of our daily prayers? The world under such circumstances of general government, where would be the use of prayer? And without the use, how shall we account for the apparent universality of it? On supposition that

every

every diftribution of good and evil, of SERMON
happinefs and mifery, is irreverfibly or- IV.
dained to take place in this life, according
to certain general laws impofed on nature,
which in no inftance whatever admit of
any alteration in our favour : what futi-
lity, what weaknefs, I had almoft faid
what folly were it, to throw up any particular petition to the Almighty for any
occafional blefling, we may ftand moft in
need of; which, to our prayers, though
ever fo ardent and importunate, on the
fuppofed exclufion of a particular providence, we know will not, cannot be
granted.

Such uncomfortable confequences as
thefe, the admiffion of a providence acting every where, and, if it act any
where, it muft act every where, pervading
every minuteft particle in nature, ever noting and directing every movement of the
moral world, effectually precludes. This
important, exhilerating truth communicates encouragement to virtuous purfuits,
G 2 . adds

adds vigour to good endeavours, beams comfort to diftrefs ; and awes the front of profligacy with a control fuperior to the menace of racks and tortures, or the check of worldly fhame.

And apart from the immediate blefl- ings, prayer draws down on the relying votary, the practice of it is calculated to improve the mind in virtue ; exalting hu- man nature by communications with the Divine. It habituates us to look up to God, as the author of all good, infufes the love of Him in our hearts, and im- prints the confcioufnefs of his perpetual prefence on our minds : which is the moft efficacious prefervative againft the admit- tance of impure thoughts, and the per- petration of flagitious actions. Thus to contemplate the Deity, and hold com- munion with him in the manner reafon directs, is ufing our intellectual facul- ties, as to the higheft reach, fo to the trueft purpofe of them. It would be difficult to affign any other good, point-
tedly

tedly and effentially good, ufe of them; and it is impoffible to affign a better.

SERMON IV.

III. To fupport the arguments already offered in proof of the obligation of religion on all beings poffeft of intellectual powers equal to thofe of man; I proceed in the third and laft place to obferve the connection, that God Almighty hath ordained between the acknowledgment of Him, expreffed in the duties of religion; and the good order of fociety, and comforts of life from thence refulting, the practice of the focial and relative duties.

Of this truth the proof muft reft chiefly on hiftorical reprefentation: and to this we may appeal in evidence, that where there has been found little fenfe of God and religion, or where the notions of religion have been greatly debafed and corrupted; there the manners of the people have been moft favage and brutifh. On the contrary, where the jufteft and moft lively fenfe of a Deity and

SERMON IV.

and providence prevailed; there the social and relative virtues have most flourished, the most worthy and generous actions have been performed, and the manners have been ever the most humane and civilifed. This is fo clear and acknowledged a truth, and fo forcibly ftruck a great Heathen, that " if " piety towards God were removed, he " declares it his opinion, that there " would be an end of all fidelity, of the " bonds of all human fociety, and even " of juftice itfelf, the fum and compre- " henfion of all moral virtues."* The reflection is worthy of a Chriftian philofopher: and, the queftion properly ftated, the foundeft divinity would with the great Roman decide on it.

The queftion is not, whether a particular thoughtful fpeculatift may not fee

* Atque haud fcio an, pietate adverfus Deos fublata, fides etiam, et focietas humani generis, et una excellentiffima virtus juftitia, tollatur.

Cic. de Nat. Deor. Lib. 1.

the

the fitnefs of many moral actions, and perform them accordingly; without regard to any other confideration, without reflecting on a prefiding, governing, remunerating, chaftifing power: though even on this reftricted ftatement of the cafe, an impartial obferver of human nature would not hefitate to declare in the negative. But the fubject of enquiry is; whether, uninfluenced by the apprehenfion, of fomething diftinct from this principle of mere fitnefs or congruity of actions to the nature of things, of fome being, on whom the exiftence of things themfelves, and confequently their natures, and the congruity of one to another, depend, the generality of men could ever poffefs fuch firm notions of good and evil, as would conftitute a fufficient principle of reftraint from the one, and impulfe to the other. And this queftion is no fooner afked, than the anfwer follows: that moft affuredly the love and dread of that SOMETHING, by whofe power the things themfelves exift, and by by whofe will the congruity of them to one another was fixed, is that principle; which acting uniformly, and univerfally, forcibly and clearly too, influences the bulk of mankind by the powerful motives of hope and fear.

And the knowledge we have of the human mind, derived from leffons of experience, inftructs us; that without fuch belief of a fupreme intelligent Being, on whom the nature of things depends, who has a power of exacting from all free agents a conformity of conduct to that law of nature, which He has eftablifhed, and will fome way or other take cognizance of them; or, in a fhorter form of words, without religion, fuch a law, as is fuppofed to arife merely from the fitnefs of things, would have but very little influence. It would be as infufficient and unimpreffive to the greateft part of mankind; as a human law, without a fanction annexed to it,

or

or the apprehenfion of a magiftrate to put it in execution.

It is poffible that fome men may poffefs fuch focial benevolence, and fuch generous fentiments of public good, as to be a law to themfelves; and at the fame time be endowed with fuch diftinguifhing judgment and acutenefs of mind, as may enable them clearly to fee, and voluntarily to act, as the beft human laws would direct them. But what is this to the bulk of mankind? We are in the prefent argument to take human nature as it generally is, and to confider what fort of belief or perfuafion has the moft prevalent and univerfal influence over it: and if we do fo, we fhall find that the rejection of religion, and its leading principles, is inconfiftent with a perfect morality on two accounts.

Firft, if there be no belief of a God, and His prefiding power, nor any expectation from that invifible Being of

future

SERMON IV.

future rewards and punishments, there cannot be in the conception of common sense, any sufficient bond of morality between man and man. And secondly, if there be really a God, that has any concern with us, or for us; a compleat morality must necessarily respect Him, as well as our intercourse with one another.

First, if indeed the actions of men were directed by instinct, and by instinct only, like the actions of brutes; and had no dependence on any invisible principle in the mind; morality would in that case be nothing else than living according to that natural instinct: nor would any kind of faith or belief be necessary. But this is not the morality of beings endued with understanding, and freedom of will; nor is it what gives them such conscioufness of the merit or demerit of their own actions, as is capable of raising pleasure or dissatisfacton within themselves, on account of them. It is
a circum-

a circumstance or consideration of a much higher nature, that acts thus: requiring reason and reflection, and some attention to things past and future, as well as the present; and supposing consequently a belief of something invisible, by which we are moved to a rational course of acting. And such consideration further implies a comparison of actions with some antecedent rule or law, for the observance or transgression of which we inwardly judge ourselves rewardable by, or accountable to, that superiour Being; who is, by some means we cannot comprehend, as conscious of what we do, as we are ourselves. It is this principle; which, as in one point of view we have found it move on stronger hinges, than moral fitness and the congruity of things, is in another that, which distinguishes reason from mere instinct, ranks mankind above the brute creation, and renders them accountable beings.

Consider

Consider secondly, the force of self-love : and that alone will be found of tendency sufficient to subvert the rectitude of moral actions; did they not depend on the acknowledgment of principles remote from sensation, and more powerful than mutual convenience. It is the secret sense we feel of an obligation to the steady performance of certain actions, founded on the belief of an intelligent legislator, who is also an inspector of our behaviour ; which gives efficacious impulse to them. For define virtue in what manner we please ; let it be the love of order, harmony, or proportion of mind ; let it be a habit or temper of living agreeably to the perfection of nature, or of acting for the good of the whole human race, of which we are but a part; call it as we may, by whatever specious name : yet the question still recurs ; who constituted this order of things : who first effected this harmony or proportion : or, who is the author of this course of things, which

we

we call the courfe of nature? for He Sermon muft be the ultimate legiflator: and IV. this law of nature, this rule of morality, which we are taught to obferve, muft be His will; directed by His fupreme authority; and muft therefore in the firft inftance refpect Him.

Under fuch perfuafion, it is his influential power, that actuates us in our determinations, and the execution of them: and not the order, fitnefs, and propriety of the things themfelves. Without the powerful co-operation of this principle, how weak would be the influence of moral confiderations! If, by an act of private injury, we could indulge a prefent gratification; eafily would the plea of felf-indulgence break through the cobweb texture of exact propriety: and weak would be the voice of mutual convenience; whenever felf-intereft interfered. It is confcience alone, that can combat temptations; and triumph over the ftrong principle of felf-love, in whatever fhape it may affault us. And confcience is folely founded

SERMON IV.

founded on a confcioufnefs of a fupreme intelligent Being, the framer of thofe laws of morality; and of our accountablenefs to Him for the breach of them. And naturally and clofely united with our belief of fuch a divine exiftence is the opinion or perfuafion, that this fupreme Being is a witnefs of what we do even in our moft fecret receffes; and confiders our actions with favour or difpleafure: for without this confideration, it would be difficult to conceive, how our own confciences fhould be affected with fhame or fatisfaction, not dependent on the eftimation of the world, but entirely our own: a fhame, though men applaud us, when we do ill; and a fatisfaction, though men cenfure us for worthy actions.

Thefe effects of confcience imply a belief of the intimate and conftant prefence of one, whofe favour or difpleafure is more to be regarded, than any outward confideration. And it hence follows,

lows, that whatever opinion fets us loofe from the reftraint of confcience, will render our juftice, fidelity, gratitude, and all other virtues refpecting our fellow creatures very precarious: and that therefore an avowed difregard of religion, and its influence, muft be neceffarily deftructive of that morality, which regards our intercourfe with one another; and fubverfive of civil fociety.

SERMON IV.

Such is the natural relation of religion to morality; of fuch importance to this is that, in force and ufe. What therefore God hath connected and joined together, not all the cafuiftry and device of man can put afunder. Morality cannot be compleat and perfect, without a difcharge of what is due to, without a regulation of behaviour, fuiting and becoming, every relation, in which we ftand to every being; the duty we owe, rifing in exigence proportionate to the excellence of the being, to whom we owe it. The firft, the moft diftinguifhed, part of
relative

Sermon IV.

relative duty therefore muſt be in proper acts of devout homage to that firſt and ſuprem. Being; from whom we derive all that we poſſeſs, even the principle, that teaches us this duty, the power of reaſon itſelf: and thoſe acts of homage conſtitute religion.

With ſuch irreſtible light doth reaſon illuſtrate the general obligation of religious duties. *Though heaven and earth paſs away*; religion, whatever the weak and the vain may affect to think of it, is a ſervice, that will continue for ever. It is the employment of ſuperior beings; and will continue, when this periſhable globe of ours ſhall be no more. There may be thoſe, their time devoted to pleaſure, or engaged by buſineſs, who affect ſurpriſe; that any ſhould be found ſo weak, as to trouble themſelves about its doctrines, or take a ſerious part in its pretenſions. But if there be a God; religion is a ſerious thing. And if its pretenſions be examined with becoming ſeriouſneſs,

seriousness, and its merits without prejudice decided on; we shall find, that to believe its doctrines, and to practice its precepts aright, is the wisest thing, that can engage a wise man's attention; and the noblest principle, that can influence his conduct. Gratitude enjoins the observance of it as a duty; and the object renders it the first and great duty. Hope warmly interests good men in its favour: and just apprehension should teach all men with reverence to regard it. The wit and ingenuity of man may have been employed against this, and that, and every mode of religion; which tends to restrain the appetites and inclinations of mankind. But we may defy the wit, and ingenuity, and malice of human nature, to produce a single argument; in disproof of the obligation of religion on all beings, possest of a degree of intelligence equal to that of man.

Knaves may detest, and fools deride, the wise man will always revere, it. Creating

ating satisfaction, it sanctions the enjoyments of life: inspiring fortitude, it renders the evils of life supportable; and opens the amplest prospect of fair and reasonable hopes. Let us hold it fast: to the fastidious sneer, and the calumnious cavil, let no false respect for politeness, or even greatness itself, deter us from *giving an answer*. And that we may at all times, and on all occasions, be ready with our best exertions to defend its sacred truths, and to evince them in our lives; May God of His infinite mercy grant, through Jesus Christ our Lord.

SERMON V.

Isaiah lix. 9.

We wait for light ; but behold obscurity: for brightness, but we walk in darkness.

THE prophet, in the beginning of this chapter, exclaims against the vices of his people ; and laments their deplorable depravation of manners, immersed as they were in the darkness of ignorance and sin. Thence stretching forward his anxious eye to the expected coming of the Messiah, destined to remove the cloud that veiled their understanding, we *wait*, says he, *for light, but still behold obscurity* ; expectant of brightness, we continue to walk in the devious path

SERMON V.

path of error and fin. At length, his mind as it were exulting in a full profpect of that day, when *the fun of righteoufnefs fhall arife, and the redeemer appear in Zion*; in the fpirit of prophecy he pronounces, that the extended world from eaft to weft fhall acknowledge his fway. *So fhall they fear*, fays he, *the name of the Lord from the weft, and his glory from the rifing of the fun : when the enemy fhall come up like a flood ; the fpirit of the Lord fhall fet up a ftandard againft him. And the redeemer fhall come to Sion ; and unto them that turn from tranfgreffion in Jacob.*

Something, fimilar to this reflection of the prophet, ftrikes us in the fecond Alcibiades of Plato : in which Socrates informs his difciple, that they were to wait for a teacher, who would inftruct them more perfectly in the duties of religion. This remarkable paffage has by an elegant writer * of our own nation

* Mr. Addifon.

been

been made the subject of criticism: and other commentators have concurred with him, in supposing it to bear some allusion to that *life and immortality*, which Jesus Christ afterwards *brought to light through his gospel*. Be that as it may; considering the obscurity and perplexity, with which the philosopher expresses himself on the subject of prayer, I think it clearly inferrible from thence, that he conceived the light of nature, or the bare apprehension of reason, insufficient to direct mankind fully and satisfactorily in that great important duty: so great and important in that wise heathen's opinion, as to require more information than the world at that time possessed.

In accommodation to minds of a certain complection, on which the authority of an eminent heathen, I know not by what kind of perverseness, has more weight than that of writers, whom we justly stile DIVINE; of the passage, to which I have above alluded, I will take

take occasion to enter into a more minute discussion. Αναγκαιον ουν εςι περιμενειν, εως αν τις μαθη ως δει προς Θεους και προς ανθρωπους διακεισθαι. * Socrates must from hence either mean to insinuate; that we were to wait for the future appearance of a person, to instruct mankind in the duty of religion, of more general knowledge, higher natural abilities, and greater reach of understanding, than himself, or any one, who had appeared before him, possessed: or, that we must wait for some person, who should for that purpose be by God particularly delegated.

In respect to his own natural abilities, and reach of understanding; it is pretty clear, our philosopher did not think very meanly of himself. Many of his cotemporaries objected to him the charge of vanity: and one in particular termed him, " of the few good men, the best;

---

* Wherefore we must be forced to wait till some one shall instruct us, how we ought to conduct ourselves towards the Gods and men.

" and

OF THE CHRISTIAN RELIGION. 119

" and of many vain ones, the vain-
" eſt."* Notwithſtanding the affected
humility of that celebrated acknowledgment, " that all he knew, was, that he
" knew nothing :" confident as he ever
appeared in the rectitude of his own opinions, and obſtinate in maintaining them,
he certainly entertained no contemptible
notion of his own fuperiour wifdom.
And the ignorance he confeſſed, ſeems
only to have been a trap to gain ap-
plauſe : or at moſt it was no other than
an ignorance of particular ſubjects, of
that phyſical knowledge, of which the
philoſophers uſed to boaſt themſelves;
ſuch as the nature of the Gods, the
principles of things, &c. And accordingly the confequence, that the ſophiſts,
or philoſophers, aſſumed from their affected fcience in thoſe ſtudies, he deriſo-
rily contraſted by an avowed ignorance
of them : quitted thoſe vain, unſatisfac-

* Σωκρατες ανδρων βελτιϛτ' ολιγων, πολλων δε
ματαιοταθ'—

SERMON V.

tory subjects of investigation, and confined his philosophical disquisitions to ethics.

Competent as he was to judge of the powers of the human mind, and reasoning from analogy, he could have little ground to expect, or even hope; that the bare strength of unassisted reason would in any individual ever reach that perfection of knowledge, which should be able to investigate the nature of God, and to ascertain the duties of man from such investigation resulting. He saw, what human reason from such researches had effected; and from thence judged, what it could do. We must therefore conclude, that he did not expect a man of that very superiour reach of understanding; which should be able, from the natural powers of human reason, to set mankind aright in their knowledge of God, and the immediate duties that relate to Him.

What then did he expect, what did he teach his disciple to look for? Plainly ly for a person endowed with powers of mind, enlarged beyond the ordinary stretch of human capacity; and delegated to the office of instructing mankind in their immediate duty to God. And as such qualification of course involved a more perfect knowledge of the Deity, than philosophy had ever taught; so likewise did it imply a more perfect practice of the duties immediately flowing from our relation to Him, than mankind had before been accustomed to observe. And such designation, and such knowledge, charactered a person charged with a divine revelation.

Sermon V.

I do not call to my assistance in this argument the foreknowledge of events, to which this philosopher occasionally made pretensions; and suppose his observation, on the reasonable expectation of a future instructor, a prophecy. I press it no further than in proof, that the wise heathen was convinced of the necessity of a revelation: and we may

be

be bold to set the opinion of the man, whom antiquity proclaimed the wisest of mankind, against all that the philosophic pride of this, or any other age, hath said or written against it. And such the opinion of Socrates, is very reconcileable with the general notions of prophecies, miracles, and mysteries; to which all nations have occasionally pretended, and attributed them to the operation of their Gods: and therefore is liable to no objection, on account of the supposed singularity of it.

From this eminent character of antiquity, let us descend to one of more modern date: from whom I have to offer an argument, though of a different nature, in point and purpose the same: I mean the learned and able author of the " Religion of Nature delineated." It is an argument, his own labours supply; and his own acknowledgment supports it. " Here, ' says that able writer, speaking of the immortality of the soul,' I be-
" gin

"gin to be very fenfible, how much I want a guide. But as the religion of nature is my theme, I muft at prefent content myfelf with that light, which nature affords."* And indeed the neceffity of such a guide, as he alludes to, his laborious inveftigation of the fubject, on which he writes, abundantly evinces. For if a knowledge of the divine nature, and man's duty to God from thence refulting, were neceffary to human happinefs; and fuch a courfe of argument, as he purfues, were the only means natural reafon pointed out for attaining to it: fo few are capable of being inftructed by fo abftrufe a method, as renders evident the further want of fome more compendious, clear, and ready means of communicating it; and demonftrates, that a revelation was neceffary for the general inftruction of mankind.

* Wollafton's Relig. of Nat. fect. 9.

Sermon V.

On the nature of the Deity, the prefent ſtate of man, and the duties incumbent on him, as deduced from the principles of cultivated reaſon, perhaps no writer ever thought ſo well, or ſo ſatisfactorily addreſſed himſelf to the underſtanding, as Wollaſton. But why hath he, or many other moderns that might be cited, thought and written of the religion of nature ſo much better, than the antients have done: except that they had a light, which thoſe wanted; the light, that chriſtianity hath holden out to them: with which many have emblazed their idol, reaſon; overlooking, like the votaries of the moon, the great ſource from whence all its light is derived? Look into the writings of the antients, and ſee how far their abilities in every branch of literature, that doth not depend on experiments, mock the feeble efforts of later ages to excel, or rival them; and then let thoſe, who can, produce a reaſon, why the moderns have written ſo much

much better on the subjects of morality and religion, than the antients have done, except the reason I have assigned.

SERMON V.

In my former discourses, I endeavoured to evince the creative, and preserving power of God; and to deduce from thence, the obligation of religion on all beings possessing intellectual faculties in a degree equal to that of man. The short question now before us is, whether the light of natural reason be sufficient to instruct us in the duties of religion; or a more express revelation of God's will in those particulars be necessary.

And in this discussion, our first object of enquiry will be, how far, on a full and fair investigation of the powers of reason, uncultivated by science, and common to mankind, they are calculated to lead us to that perfect knowledge of God; which is necessary to produce a corresponding knowledge of the duties

we

we owe Him; such a firm undoubting knowledge, as shall have a proper influence on our practice.

I propose in the second place, to confirm the result of such enquiry; by evincing from facts and experience, how far unassisted reason hath gone in promoting divine knowledge, and religious practice, among the characters most reputed for wisdom in the heathen world.

And in conclusion, we shall thirdly find it, from those enquiries, follow; that the best and purest system of religion, which unassisted reason can frame, will be defective in perspicuity, efficacy, and universality.

I. For the more clear elucidation of the argument I am now pursuing, it may be necessary to explain the terms. By the religion attainable by the powers of reason, is understood natural religion: a term used in distinction from revelation.

revelation. And by NATURAL RELIGION SERMON V.
I confequently underftand, not a fenfe
of religious duty ftamped upon the human mind, and judging with innate difcrimination of right and wrong: for, in this acceptation of the terms, the fenfe of religious duty would be general and uniform, however the practice was. But the terms, in my conception of them, denote an obligation of duty, arifing from our relation to our Creator, to which the mind is fuppofed to give an unerring affent; thereto induced by a natural aptitude, and congruity of our ideas to the divine nature and attributes. And thus confidered, the mind muft perfectly comprehend the nature of the object, and ground of that relation, from whence thofe duties flow.

In what degree of perfection the mind might originally have come out of the hands of its Creator, how clear in its decifions of right and wrong, how competent to judge of moral relations, to
fway

SERMON V.

sway, and direct, our actions; while conscience assisted as a faithful monitor, unbiassed by prejudice, not warped by bad example; is a matter of too much disputation, thereon to build an argument. With whatever readiness of mind I may assent to the doctrine of primæval perfection;* I mean not to argue from it, as a fact. We are to consider the powers of the human mind as we now find them, and as known experience from history represents them.

From the creative and preserving power of God, it has been already proved, that all religious duties flow: the mind therefore must be perfectly clear in its conception of those truths, in order perfectly to ascertain the duties that result from them. How far competent natural reason, that is, reason in its uncultivated, unimproved state, reason operating

* Vid. Concio de Statu Paradisiaco.

on the mind in the mafs of mankind, is to the difcovery and comprehenfion of thofe two great and fundamental truths, on which hinge all the duties of religion ; the train of reafoning already ufed on thofe fubjects will clearly evince. And while it is demonftrable, that without a full, and clear, and comprehenfive knowledge of thofe fundamental doctrines, it is impoffible to know the duties that refult from them : it will follow, that a fhorter, and eafier method of inculcating the knowledge of thofe doctrines, is neceffary to a general comprehenfion of the duties fo refulting ; as a clear comprehenfion of the duties, is neceffary to the practice of them.

With regard to the exiftence of the Deity, I would not have it underftood, as from hence collected ; that this momentous doctrine, the foundation of all religion, is abfolutely undifcoverable by human reafon : confcious as I am of the rational evidence, by which it may be demonftrated

SERMON V.

demonſtrated. But the general prevalence of aſſent to this great truth, in all ages of the world, hath, I conceive, been rather owing to an innate idea of ſuch an exiſtence, than a conviction of it by reaſon and argument. It may with certainty be affirmed, that the common capacity of mankind, is not capable of making this diſcovery by the mere force of reaſon : becauſe it is only to be made in the uſe of ſuch abſtracted ideas, and ſuch abſtruſe reaſoning and manner of deduction, as is far beyond the reach and powers of mind, obſervable in the generality of men. And it would be unneceſſary to repeat the arguments, that have been already produced in proof of that doctrine ; or to offer ſuch others, as might be propoſed ; to evince, that the plaineſt arguments of conviction, of which the nature of the ſubject is capable, it is above the level of an ordinary capacity, to frame, or even to comprehend the proceſs and force of them.

The

The same conclusion is equally in proof, respecting the governing and presiding power of the Deity. Yet it must also, in regard to this doctrine, be acknowledged; that there are topics in great variety, which, if properly attended to, and by the inquisitive and cultivated mind pursued, afford ample conviction of the reality of a divine providence. And the evidence, which such arguments carry with them, has obtained the assent of the wisest, the most learned, and the best men; among those, who possessed not the advantages of revelation. But they are not arguments, that can be pursued by the generality of mankind: they are not so obvious, so short, and clear; as to stamp that conviction on the rude, unlettered, vulgar mind; which vulgar minds require. The difficulties of reducing the proof of this great truth to any demonstrative and scientific evidence are such, as not only exceed the utmost reach of capacity in the illiterate multitude; but such, as lie

SERMON V.

lie not very level to thofe even of penetration and learning, who may not have accuftomed themfelves to inveftigations and ftudies of that kind.

Under fuch difadvantages, well might the grofs of mankind, whole countries, run into wild idolatries and vain conceits: trembling under ideal apprehenfions of evil, and miftaking the fountain of all good. Hence proftrations that degraded, and pollutions that depraved human nature: hence the libidinous rites inftituted in honour of the Gods, whofe nature and whofe pleafures their grovling votaries held of a piece with their own: and hence the practifers of every vice were taught to juftify their conduct by the example of fome of their Gods: hence the blind dread of offended powers, and altars ftained with human blood, to avert the effects of divine difpleafure: and hence, in fine, the verieft works of Hell, done under a blind pretence of pleafing Heaven.

Indeed

SERMON V.

Indeed what better effect could mere, unaffifted, human reafon have been expected to produce in the world: indecifive and unfatisfactory as its powers have, on the moft accurate inveftigation of them, been found; when employed on thofe elevated fubjects, the nature of the Deity, and the duties of man refulting from his relation to Him? Nor is fuch light incompetent to direct the mafs of mankind only, the ignorant and vulgar, in their duty to the Deity; but even the wife and learned, who had no better guide, thofe who had made the acquifition of knowledge the bufinefs of their lives; even thofe men we fhall find confirming the refult of the preceding enquiry: as I propofed in the fecond place to exemplify, and from facts and experience to evince, how far they in their refpective ages went, in promoting divine knowledge, and religious practice.

II. The firft great authority I will cite, was Anaxagoras; who appears to have

SERMON V.

have been the firft materialift on record in the world. He fuppofed matter to have been felf-exiftent, a rude chaotic mafs: from whence he raifes a fublimated principle, which he ftiles Intelligence, who fought this ftubborn mafs; and the iffue of the conflict was the fair frame and order of things, which we behold. From fuch an idea of the Supreme Being, we may expect a confiftent notion of the duties of religion. And fo it was: as may be collected from his anfwer to a very important queftion, and much to the purpofe of our prefent inveftigation. The queftion was, " for " what purpofe man was created ?" and our wife man's anfwer was, " to con- " template the Sun, Moon, and Hea- " vens." Vain, futile philofopher ! And is this the vaft extent, to which reafon will foar ? Afk the poor unlettered difciple of Chrift the queftion ; and he will return a very different anfwer. He will tell thee, man was made, to proclaim his great Creator's praife ;

with

with heart-felt raptures to adore that power and goodnefs, which called him into exiftence; to endeavour in his proper ftation, by an interefted difcharge of the focial and relative duties, to contribute to the general happinefs of the creation, to watch and to fubdue each irregular ftart of paffion, to purify and fit the foul for a ftate of higher blifs.

Examine the notions of Ariftippus, and the Cyrenaic fect, concerning the Deity: and what do they tend to inculcate; but principles of Atheifm, and polytheiftic practice: an accommodating creed, without any influence on our life and actions: no conception of benefits received from God, nor of duties on the part of man exacted in acknowledgment of them. They had no general line of conduct: but each was ready with quaint apothegms * to defend

* Habeo Laida; non habeor a Laide.
Vid. Cic. in Epift. et 2. de Fin.

the practices, to which inclination refpectively led him. Each was a law unto himfelf; gluttonous, licentious, oftentatious or mean, as they felt themfelves individually by humour, habit, and difpofition addicted.

Ariftotle, than whom the fchools of philofophy never boafted a more nice enquirer into the nature of things, acknowledged indeed the immateriality of the Divine Being, and his providence too; but limited that providence to the charge of the cœleftial bodies, which he fuppofed by fympathy to influence and direct the courfe of the world, we inhabit: an idea this, which removes the Deity at a diftance from us; and is therefore a principle ill-calculated, whereon to ground religious duties. *

Plato caught a glimmering of light from the father of moral philofophy.

* Vid. Diog. Laert. Vit. Philofoph.

He

He affigned the direction of human affairs immediately to the care of the Gods: and feemed to have a more adequate conception of the nature of the Deity, of the human mind, and other truths connected with thofe fublime fubjects, even than the inquifitive Ariftotle himfelf. But he had travelled into Ægypt in queft of knowledge: might there have gleaned fome fcattered fragments of traditional truths, which the Jews in their long commoration in that country had left behind them; and derived the fuperiour illumination of his mind from a ftronger light, than unaffifted reafon affords.

What fhall we fay of Socrates? That he conceived an idea of the unity of the Deity: whom he infulted by a weak adherence to a ridiculous fyftem of polytheifm.

I will not rake farther into the follies and extravagances of a number of other fages;

SERMON V.

sages; who took upon them the arduous talk of inftructing mankind in the knowledge of God, the nature of the human mind, and the duties of life from the relation of man to his creator arifing. The preceding reflections will fufficiently evince this refulting truth: that the natural powers of the uninformed mind are not competent to that clear comprehenfion of God and providence; which is neceffary to eftablifh fuch conviction, as fhall produce amongft mankind a uniform and confiftent practice of religious duties.

This has been proved on the incontrovertible authority of fact and experience, in the varying and doubtful opinions, not of the rude illiterate vulgar; nor yet of chiefs and ftatefmen, whofe minds may have been fuppofed too much engaged in fcenes of active life, to have allowed leifure for fober fpeculative purfuits; but of thofe learned and beft-informed characters, who had facrificed
all

all worldly avocations to the ſtudy of wiſdom, and made the acquiſition of knowledge not only the chief, but the ſole buſineſs of their lives.

III. But ſuppoſing the opinions of philoſophic men to have been more uniform and conſiſtent, than we have found them: ſtill a religion deduced from them would want, as was obſerved in the third and laſt place, perſpicuity, efficacy, and univerſality.

I. It muſt want perſpicuity; conſiſting, as it has been ſhewn, in a long train of abſtract reaſoning: which to different perſons would appear more or leſs obvious, as individuals are more or leſs perſpicacious, apprehenſive, and acute. Thoſe arguments likewiſe would be always liable to miſconceptions and miſconſtruction; and diffidence in opinion would produce diverſity in practice. The fundamental truths of religion muſt be plain and clear: a direct declaration of facts,

facts, not supported by abstruse reasoning; but by, what would constitute a much firmer foundation, a direct appeal to the senses in the performance of miracles. The doctrine, in this case proposed to be believed, is a plain assertion: and my assent is grounded on what I feel, or hear, or see. Thus, if our reason can comprehend, that facts may be as they are represented; if our senses be convinced, that they are so; this is all the satisfaction, the mind can require: and this is a conviction suited to every mind.

II. In respect to its efficacy, as the doctrines, on which such a religion rests, must consist of very disputable points, and doubtful disquisitions : they would not carry with them conviction strong enough to influence the practice of those, to whom they are addressed ; scarcely of those, who themselves might propose them. They might believe them : but belief and conviction are very different principles,

principles, and will be found on practice to have very different effects. Elſe the great heathen philoſopher, above alluded to, at the awful hour of diſſolution, when he was going to meet that ineffably great and glorious Exiſtence, whom his conception had figured to him as the Creator and Preſerver of Heaven and Earth, would not have ventured to inſult Him with neglect; and, in weak and ſervile compliance with his country's ſilly ſuperſtitions, direct a ſacrifice to be offered to an imaginary individual of a ridiculous polytheiſtic tribe. Would a converted chriſtian, under the ſame circumſtance of prejudice in favour of his country's ceremonious rites, at ſuch awful period have been induced by any conſideration to trample on the crofs of Chriſt? This is not a queſtion of ſpeculation; the affirmative of which on one ſide is as good, as the negative on the other: we can produce facts and experience in a hundred inſtances, to prove he would not.

III. And

III. And laftly, fuch a religion muft want univerfality: for it is a religion calculated not for the generality of mankind, but for a nation of philofophers. For thofe philofophers, were they ever fo throughly perfuaded of the truth of it themfelves, could not explain it to the ignorant multitude: they could never bring thofe arduous doctrines of refined fpeculation to a level with rude uncultivated minds. And though, from the reputation of their wifdom and knowledge, they fhould poffefs fufficient influence with the vulgar, to obtain a tacit confent to the doctrines they taught: as they could propofe them with no other force, than merely the weight of their own private opinions; they could be fuppofed to have little influence on the lives and morals of thofe, to whofe inferiour underftandings they were addreffed. Stooping with pliant minds to their opinions, fome might believe; others would doubt; and, as fuch a religion muft depend on deductions of reafon,

others

others again would form different con- SERMON
clufions. Self-love and felf-fatisfaction, V.
under the guidance of natural inclination, would individually communicate
different appearances to doctrines of mere
opinion : and fcarcely one fingle point
of duty would be received with fuch
concurrent confidence and common affent; as to influence practice, againft
prefent intereft, the follicitation of pleafure, the indulgence of eafe.

But if, after all that has been urged,
we are ftill to be told, " that a wife and
good God cannot impofe on mankind
any thing relating to religion, that may
not be difcovered by the human mind
without the affiftance of *foreign* inftruction, or that is not immediately founded
in the nature of things:"* having fhewn,
from the greateft authorities in the moft
polifhed parts of the ancient world, that
the cafe is otherwife; that certain duties

* Chriftianity as old as the Creation.

SERMON V.

are required of mankind, founded on doctrines and relations, which natural reason does not clearly make known: I might afk, in turn, in what period of the world it was generally otherwife; when thofe characters exifted, who, by the natural powers of the mind, difcovered the doctrines and duties of pure religion? And I know but one fatisfactory reply that could be made; which would be, by confronting hiftorical evidence with hiftory.

There is an antient hiftory, that informs us of the primæval ftate of man: when he lived in perfect innocence and happinefs. In that ftate indeed he muft have been poffeffed of a perfect knowledge of his duty, "without any foreign inftruction." For without knowing it, he could not perform it: without performing it, he could not have been perfectly innocent: and unlefs perfectly innocent, he could not have been perfectly happy. Thus exactly confonant with the fentiment,

OF THE CHRISTIAN RELIGION. 145

ment, which from the lip of fcepticifm
I have juſt cited, do we find this very
antient hiſtory defcribe the primitive
ſtate and condition of mankind. Agreeable to it, God is reprefented as impofing on man no duty, of which he did
not know and comprehend the force.

The account of human nature and
human manners, which that hiſtory fupplies, informs us, that *though God created man perfect, he had found out many devices.*
That is, that he poffeffed at his creation
powers of mind, competent to difcern
what was right, and fufficient rectitude
of inclination to prompt him to purfue
it. But that, notwithſtanding fuch competence to know, and ability to perform,
his duty, he had deviated in his conduct
into many devices; into pofitive acts of
difobedience : that a deterioration of his
nature fucceeded ; that his underſtanding
became obfcured, and a fenfe of right and
wrong lefs fenfibly affected him. And,
confiſtent with this hiſtorical narrative,
K the

Sermon V.

the proofs, that have been above offered, extracted chiefly from the antient biographer* of those characters, whose learning and love of wisdom obtained to them the distinguished appellation of philosophers, abundantly evince; that in the deteriorated, depraved state of human nature, they were acquainted neither with the doctrines, nor duties, of pure religion.

In consideration of such experienced corruption, such deterioration of human nature, this volume proceeds to unfold the dispensations of Divine Providence; and explain those mysteries, that meet in the moral conduct of mankind. It instructs us, that to supply the defect in the natural light of reason, God promised, and according to his promise gave, mankind an additional light; or, to preserve the words of the author in the sentiments quoted above, *a foreign*

* Diogenes Laertius.

instruc-

OF THE CHRISTIAN RELIGION. 147

inftruction; * conveyed in fo clear and explicit terms and manner, that nothing is wanting to the comprehenfion of it, but an eye that will fee, and a heart difpofed to underftand.

SERMON V.

I have mentioned this hiftory, and this little abftract from it, only as the fuggeftion of an object worth invefti- gating: as it may tend to reconcile to truth, and to explain the favourite opinion of thofe, who affert that God muft have endowed man with natural powers of mind, fufficient to enable him to know His will, and to practife it. If the truth of it, as relating to a primæval ftate of perfection, be queftioned; I might, in fupport of fuch doctrine, cite antient poets and philofophers, of moft eminence in the heathen world, inculcating the fame opinion †. If the prefumed authority of that volume be treated with an affected air of ridicule; we may tell thofe

* See page 143.
† Vide Concio de Statu Paradifiaco.

K 2   who

who treat it thus, and it would furprize many, who take their fhadowy religion on the credit of others, to be told; that fome of the ableſt and moſt learned men, this country ever produced, have not only been private believers, but public defenders of the doctrinal truths, which that volume contains. And it would be equally mortifying on their part, to obferve to them; that the adverfaries of revealed religion, in this country, have been generally men of very fuperficial learning; fuch as have feldom waded into the depths of fcience, or contributed to the advancement of erudition and knowledge in any material article: contenting themfelves, by an affectation of fingularity, a love of cavil, and parade of words, with a cheaper purchafe of fame. That by men of this defcription we may never fuffer ourfelves to be laughed out of our religion, out of our prefent comfort, and our future hopes, may God of His infinite mercy grant, &c.

SERMON VI.

John iv. 2.

Salvation is of the Jews.

TO ascertain, how far natural reason was competent to discover the duties of pure religion, was the object of my last discourse: which, flowing from a just apprehension of the divine nature, and the relation in which we stand to the Supreme Being, must depend for their propriety and uniformity on the reach of our ideas, as directed to that sublime subject; and the equal extent of them. If they be inadequate to the subject, the duties will be imperfect; if they vary in individuals, larger and more comprehensive in some than others, the

K 3   rule

Sermon VI

rule of duty founded on them muft be vague and varying. And from the preceding inveftigation it was by proof and example evinced ; that not only the mafs of mankind, but even the wife and learned, entertained very different notions of the divine nature, and had varying and very imperfect ideas of the relative duties of man to his Creator : that, from fuch difcrepance of opinion, no general rule of practice could be formed ; nor on the moral conduct of mankind could fuch imperfect knowledge, as they poffeffed, of God and religion, have fufficient influence.

Many of them conceived falfe and injurious notions of God : and the opinions even of thofe, who might be nearer the truth, were too much involved in doubts and obfcurity, to be efficacious in gaining them to a ftrict and uniformly religious life ; much lefs in promoting the practice of religion among the multitude. Yet the creative and
preferving

preserving goodness of God, it was in- ferred, * demand from beings endowed with a degree of reason, equal to that of man, a return of rational service ; or, in other words, the observance of religious duties. And to practise religion in purity and truth, we must understand its doctrines and commands. We must comprehend them clearly, we must be throughly convinced of the divine authority, that instituted and enjoined them : or they will have no efficacy on our lives. If therefore the light of nature be not competent to this effect; God, who conferred that light on us, as he easily could, so we must conclude as readily would, confer on us a supplemental aid, some stronger and clearer light. How such supplemental aid may be conferred, we will next proceed to enquire.

He, who endowed the cultivated mind with sufficient powers, by long and laborious

* See page 86, &c.

borious operations of reason to learn to know Him, can no doubt as easily communicate to the mind such knowledge of Himself some shorter way, by immediate illumination; a ray of intuitive knowledge, lighting to certain truths, to any truths, that are not above the natural grasp of that mind. For instance, the mind can conceive the idea of a first cause, infinitely active and powerful. This knowledge may be acquired, through the medium of a long chain of reasoning: or it may be communicated to that mind supernaturally and immediately. But to comprehend the manner of God's existence, exceeds the reach of human intelligence. This is a degree of knowledge, which cannot be acquired by any exertions of reason: nor can it be immediately and supernaturally communicated to the human mind. For to receive such degree of knowledge, the mind itself must be altered, its capacity enlarged, its nature changed: but change the nature of the mind,

mind, and you unmake the man. Hence
then we find no apparent difficulty in
conceiving a fupernatural communication of knowledge : and we alfo learn,
what kind and degree of knowledge
may be to the mind thus fupernaturally
and inftantaneoufly communicated ; viz.
any knowledge, which the mind by the
operation of reafon is capable in a natural way of acquiring. And the man
thus divinely illuminated is as capable
of communicating to others fuch illumination of knowledge, as he who may
have acquired it in the ordinary way :
and indeed with greater weight ; for he
feels it, and communicates it as a divine
impreffion, and therefore an incontrovertible truth.

But the mere belief of internal illuminations, is no proof that we poffefs
them : for thofe fancied feelings, that
are boafted by many of weak heads and
warm imaginations, are as impreffive as
real ones : we may be deceived by them
ourfelves,

Sermon
VI.

SERMON ourselves, and thereby led to deceive
VI. others. There is need therefore of some external proof of the truth and reality of our pretensions: and no surer or more satisfactory one can be conceived, than the performance of acts, which exceed the ordinary powers of nature. They are direct appeals to the senses; and when the experience of internal illuminations is attended with such characters of external evidence; it acts with all the force of conviction truth can give, and has a claim to rational assent. Indeed it is capable of proof, that internal illuminations cannot exist, unattended with some external character of authenticity. For whom would the person, who could produce no other proofs of the reality of his mental illuminations, than his own feelings, convince? And without the power of convincing others, what would be the use of such illuminations? And without a use, or purpose, and a good one too, it is hard to conceive that God, who does nothing in

vain,

vain, should distinguish any individual with such supernatural gifts and powers.

SERMON VI.

The possibility of divine illuminations being thus evinced, and the characteristic marks distinguished, which authorise their currency, and establish their truth; the next point of enquiry is, whether any such illumination, revealing God's will in a more express, and clear, and concise manner, than by arguments and abstruse reasoning, hath ever taken place; and whether the purpose to be promoted by it was such, as would justify the divine interposition.

Nations and countries have not varied more in their civil, than in their religious institutions. Some nations, in their opinions of the divine nature, have divided it into a multiplicity of Gods: and some have materialised it; for the Creator mistaking, and worshipping, his works. Great and vain men have taken advantage of this general principle of religion,

ligion, which poffeffes the minds of all mankind; pretended the ufeful arts they invented, or their fucceffes in war, thofe to have been the communications of their Gods, and thefe atchieved by their affiftance: and from thence obtained, amongft their refpective countrymen, the opinion of being the diftinguifhed favourites of Heaven, and after death the honours of Deification.

The moft antient people, of which prophane hiftory profeffes to give us any account, are the Ægyptians and Chaldæans: and of their hiftories the earlieft period, to which we can refer, is the time of Sefoftris; about a thoufand, or, as fome contend, fifteen hundred, years before Chrift. And the earlieft reprefentation, which the page of hiftory holds out to us, of their religion and morals, difcovers them to have been immerfed in the groffeft idolatry. Nor do the records of Greece afford us a more advantageous account of their moft

priftine

pristine state. The imaginary existences of deceased men were the only Gods, they knew ; their will, when living, the only rule of morals the people acknowledged ; and their vices, after they were dead, the sanction of incest, ambition, and outrage of every kind.

SERMON VI.

If, amidst such an idolatrous world, there were a people, who thought and acted otherwise ; who acknowledged one only God, the Creator and Upholder of all things ; who paid Him a consistent service ; who lived in the habitual practice of duties resulting from a proper knowledge, a love, a fear, a reverence of Him : we can account for such knowledge, and such consistent practice, only two ways. One is, that those people must have been more wise and pious, not only than any other nation under Heaven ; but than a nation, could such an one be conceived, composed of individuals the most distinguished for superiour wisdom and erudition,

erudition, a select nation of philosophers. Or else, that extraordinary degree of knowledge, they possessed, must have been communicated to them some other way; than by the mere exertion of the natural powers of reason. The first of these suppositions certainly was not the case. The Jews assuredly did not possess more learning, than the rest of the nations, among whom they lived: but it may on the contrary be asserted, that in the early periods of that nation, before their emigration from Ægypt, indeed till the reigns of David and Solomon, they possessed less. The highest encomium on their great prince and legislator respecting his erudition was, that he *was skilled in all the learning of the Ægyptians*: a direct acknowledgment, that he had not acquired his learning and knowledge from his own countrymen; but from a people more learned and intelligent than they were; and of course more capable of instructing him. The latter hypothesis must be therefore the true one: and

and it confequently follows, that their knowledge of God and religion had been communicated to them by fome fhorter, clearer, more convincing, more influencing way.

And as fuch fupernatural interpofition of God, in revealing his will to mankind by an immediate illumination of the mind, that is, by infpiration, muft have a fufficient affignable caufe : if we enquire the purpofe to be promoted in the inftance before us ; we fhall find it the nobleft, the moft important, that can be conceived worthy to engage the divine interference. It was to keep alive in the human mind the almoft extinguifhed principles of true religion ; to teach and inforce the knowledge of God, and the relative duties of all rational beings from thence refulting : that the moft elevated point of human knowledge ; and this the firft great duty of mankind. In pity to human weaknefs and infirmity, which to the moft vile and abject prof-

trations

trations had reduced the original perfect and dignified character of man, was this revelation made. Formed with a mind competent to know, and taught to commune with, his Creator; still bearing the faint impreffion of His goodnefs, but loft to every proper idea of His nature; he had humbled himfelf to the worfhip of an animal, a plant, a ftock, or a ftone. And from that abyfs of ignorance to recover and reinftate him in the rank of intelligence, he once poffeffed; was a purpofe abundant to juftify the interpofition of God, in employing the only means equal to fuch an effect.

But befides the end or purpofe affignable for fuch divine interference: fome further evidence of the reality of it, as hath been already premifed, is wanting. And no evidence can be produced fo eafy of conception, and fo affuredly to be depended on, as miracles: the poffibility of which having in a * former dif-

---
* See Sermon xi.

courfe

OF THE CHRISTIAN RELIGION. 161

course been evinced, * we will now en- Sermon
ter farther into the subject, and consider VI.
the circumstances necessary to authen-
ticate the performance of them.

By a miracle, we understand a sensible effect exceeding the known powers
of nature. But as we are utterly ignorant, how far the powers of beings, good
or bad, in superior classes of intelligence,
may extend; we cannot be certain, that
some phœnomena, which appear, and
are, to us really miraculous, may not
have resulted from their agency. And
it therefore follows, that miracles are
not separately, and in themselves, proofs,
that the workers of them are delegated
messengers of God. Yet as it is highly
repugnant to all our natural notions of
the divine goodness, to suppose that He
can leave men, who desire to know and
follow truth, destitute of the necessary

* See Sermon ii. p. 38, &c.

L means

SERMON VI.

means of difcriminating it from falfehood; it alfo follows, that there muft ever be fome difcernible traits and adjuncts, which mark and manifeft His interpofition. By what characters then are the miracles of true religion diftinguifhable from deceptions? By plain peculiarities, as I conceive, in their nature, manners, and tendency.

We are, it is confeffed, ignorant how far the power of evil fpirits may extend: but we know how far it cannot extend: we know it is infinitely inferiour to the power of God. Upon this principle, reafon, concurring with fcripture, appropriates fome wonderful acts of a particular kind to God Himfelf, and as proceeding only from Him: fuch as the prediction of diftant contingencies, depending upon the wills of free agents; and the ability with unerring knowledge of difclofing the privacy of human thoughts. That an idea prevailed in the heathen world, of the poffibility of thofe facts,

facts, appears from the endeavours used to establish the belief of them. What else was the pretence of their oracles? How vain and futile such attempts, I will not go about to prove. I will not intrude on your time by exposing the futile boasts of augury, and the vain pretensions of such pillars of the art, as Nævius: his arrogated knowledge of human thoughts, a plain, palpable, collusive juggle between his prince and him, to procure confidence from an ignorant multitude, without authentic vouchers, without sufficient end;

———————— " Nodus non NUMINE dignus."

An observation this, which leads me to consider some attendant circumstances in extraordinary acts, as constituting another proof of their immediate procedure from God. As, when they are public, performed openly before great numbers; and when the result of them is a notoriously permanent effect. These, if not equally infallible marks of the

SERMON VI.

finger of God, as the super-natural operation itself, are corroborating proofs, amongst others, that they proceed from divine power; that they are true and real miracles, and not, like those ascribed to magicians, oracles, and heathen augurs, the illusions of artifice, and pretensions of falshood and imposture.

The tendency of those wonderful acts, or the purposes for which they were wrought, is likewise, as hath been intimated, a test of their divinity. A miracle, that tends to no purpose, or to a bad one, is on those very accounts suspicious. If the all-wise and good God ever suspend, or alter, the established course of nature; it must be for some wise and good cause: for some important end, which could not otherwise be obtained. It must be immediately, or ultimately, for the removal of some pernicious and spreading errors, or the confirmation of some momentous truths; in order to render mankind wiser and better.

ter. When therefore we are convinced, that miracles bear the characters above represented, are also attended with the marks and distinctions just described; and that the ends, which in this enumeration of circumstantial evidence I have specified, are intended by them : we may be assured, that they proceed not from wicked spirits, such supposition implying a contradiction in ideas ; as it is contrary to their nature to promote good : and by consequence, that they are, and can be, only from God.

After these premised observations, let us proceed to take a general view of the revelation made to the Jews. All nations have in their respective religious institutions pretended to prophecies, miracles, and mysteries ; and considered such powers and discoveries to have been conferred on favoured individuals by the predilection and good-will of their Gods : which, though it do not prove, that the world in every special part of it has had a revelation; yet plainly evinces, that, by the judgment of the whole world, there was reafon to expect, and believe one. Till the time of Mofes, the records of hiftory were traditional: at leaft, we have no affurance, till then, of any written ones. He firft digefted the antient accounts of hiftorical facts; and committed them to writing. And in regard to the narrative of antient facts, which he delivers, and had received from tradition; it is to be obferved, that thofe traditions, from the longevity of the Ante-diluvians, had not in the courfe of defcent paffed through many reporters: * and the hiftorian feems to have related them without the leaft prejudice or partiality to himfelf or his nation. Nor doth tradition, permit 'em to obferve, carry an inconfiderable weight with it; or claim a moderate degree of affent, when there appears nothing to confront, or difprove it. And this is

---

* See Pafcal's Thoughts.

fo

so far the case in the instance before us, that succeeding historians have in general points followed Moses's relation. They have followed him in his record of the creation of the world from a rude chaotic mass; of a paradisiacal age; of the deterioration of the world, through the vices of mankind; of an universal deluge.

From the diluvian period, this history informs us, that in one particular family, that family which survived the general catastrophe, the belief of the unity of God, creator and preserver of the world, obtained: that in one particular branch of that family, amidst its various migrations, in its prosperous and depressed state, whether independent, or in bondage, amidst idolatrous people, oppressed by the tyranny of idolatrous masters, it still retained, and of all the nations of the world alone maintained, that doctrine. It was this doctrine, that united them so closely to one another, and so continuedly separated

rated them from all the world; as in itfelf forms a perpetual miracle.

In the time of Mofes, this family was increafed to a numerous people: and as they had before been feparated from the reft of the world by their religious principles, they were then to be divided from it in fituation, and by an appropriated inheritance; to be delivered from fervitude, and become a diftinct and independent nation. For that purpofe the God, whom they ferved, raifed them up a deliverer; and empowered him, by a fignal difplay of miraculous powers, to lead out from amidft a powerful and warlike nation an oppreffed, unarmed, defencelefs multitude: who were thus led forth, feparated, and fupported, to preferve, and diffufe among the reft of the world, the almoft obliterated notions of true Theifm, and the pure worfhip of the One God. And if any purpofe, if any end, could juftify the fupernatural interpofition of Almighty God in the difplay display of miracles, this unquestionably did.

The religion of the Jews had been hitherto plain and simple: consisting in the knowledge of the Divine Unity, and the nature of that spiritual worship, which was due to Him. But the people were now to become a great and powerful nation: and their religion, destined within its pale to comprehend, and to bless the whole world, was now to take a new form; its essentials to be fenced with rites, and ceremonies, and usages, which had a further aspect than Moses saw, and led to a wider extent. Whatever of allegory there may possibly be in some part of that prophet's writings, and such there probably is; it militates not against the fundamental truth of the relation: the facts represented under these allegories are plain; and have, as well as the more nude representation of things, an unquestionable claim to our assent. And in his general detail of facts, so allegorised and represented, it may be further observed,

SERMON
VI.
observed, that some of the gravest and best informed philosophers of antiquity have followed him.

This religion resolves itself into a triple division: the prophetic, moral, and ceremonial: they are well designed parts in one great building; each of distinct purpose, and design; and all necessary to the perfection of the whole. The prophecies stamp on it the character of divinity: without the moral part, as a rule of conduct it would be defective: and the ceremonial part illustrates the prophetic.

As to the prophetic declarations of Moses, and the succession of prophets, that followed him, they have in the most exact and unequivocal manner been fulfilled: down from the first prophecy of *the woman's seed, which should bruise the serpent's head*; to that dreadful monition of the future desolation of their city; with the aggravating circumstance of the people being reduced to such extremity
of

of diftrefs, as to be forced to *eat the flesh of their sons and their daughters:* a prophecy, which was dreadfully fulfilled at the fiege of Jerufalem by Titus. Examine other predictions, refpecting more recent times; and you will find fome fulfilled, and others every day fulfilling.

SERMON VI.

The moral part, an univerfal rule of conduct, was to continue the fame always and every where: cuftom cannot change it, time cannot render it obfolete, nor will even the plea of neceffity excufe the obfervance of it. *Though heaven and earth pafs away, not one jot, or one tittle, of the moral law shall fail.*

But the ritual and ceremonial part of that religion was figurative and typical; even in the perfon of the great legiflator himfelf. He was fent by God to be a deliverer. But out of Sion, as the apoftle argues, came the true Deliverer: a Deliverer in that extenfive fenfe of the word, in which the Meffiah is defcribed by

Sermon VI.

by the prophets: a Deliverer, through whom all the world should be saved. The institution of sacrifices, which originated in the earliest ages of the world, and in every part of it prevailed, apart from reverence to that great sacrifice destined to be made in the person of the Messiah, is of all strange practices the most inexplicable. On any other ground considered, the custom of offering up slaughtered animals, to expiate human offences, must appear to have proceeded from the wildest notions, the imagination of man had ever conceived. But an enthusiastic conceit, without any reasonable pretence, seldom lasts long; and never could become universal. The universality of the practice therefore adds to the improbability, shall I call it, or impossibility of it; except founded in reason and truth. And the reason and the truth of it can only consist, in its aspect to the great sacrifice destined in Christ; and are evidenced in the long continuation of the practice prefigured.

The

SERMON VI.

The deliverance from the bondage of Ægypt is a type of the deliverance of mankind from the bondage of sin; each preceded by similar circumstances, one of the Paschal feast, and the other of Christ's last supper; the one plainly prefigured by the other, and both conspiring to mark, beyond the possibility of mistake, the grand ante-type of our redemption. What do their frequent ablutions signify, but what Christ seems to allude to; the purity of the heart? *Ye hypocrites,* says he, *ye are very careful in washing the outside of the cup and platter; but within ye are full of all uncleanliness.* That is, ye blind, who can carry your eye no farther than the type; than the mere ordinance, perfectly insignificant without a reference to the reason, the ground, and the substantiality of it. In short, it is not difficult, in most of their ceremonies, to discover an aspect to a future reality: those temporary institutions tending, like so many elucidating circumstances, to point out that Redeemer;

deemer; in whom they were taught to expect a final and compleat falvation.

And thofe external obfervances whofe references and allufions lay lefs open to explanation, fo rigidly exacted, and fo ftrictly obferved, do in no fmall degree contribute to ftamp on it the evidence of divine authority. Burthenfome as they certainly are, ridiculous as in fome inftances they may appear, filly and fantaftical as they have fometimes been held; even thofe rites and ceremonies, contribute like under-parts to the one great defign; the proof, that it is of more than human inftitution. Befides the typical reference fome of them contain: others have been obferved * to ftrike at idolatrous cuftoms; and were calculated to guard the true Theift from heathen practices, and every tendency to idol fervice.

* Vid. Spencer de Leg. Heb.

And

And confidered alfo in another view, they equally demand our admiration, and claim a rational affent to the divine original of the inftitution. For what private man can be fuppofed, without the authority of ftation, unfupported by the arm of power, to have had fuch influence over a whole nation ; as, by his bare recommendation, to induce them to burthen themfelves with fuch a grievous load of vain rites and futile ordinances, vain and futile if confidered only with a view to the inftitutions themfelves, as the Jews bound themfelves to obferve ? What individual, unlefs divinely authorifed, would have prefumed to perfuade a whole nation, to abridge themfelves of fo many gratifications, which the reft of the world enjoyed; and to fubmit implicity to fuch reftraints, particularly refpecting the obfervance of the Sabbath, as might be, and was often really, prejudicial to them not only in a private, but a public capacity ? And, with lefs than divine fupport, what
individual

Sermon VI.

Sermon VI.

individual could in so arduous an undertaking have prevailed? What other motive, what weaker authority, what inferiour power, can human sagacity conceive; of sufficient urgency, to influence a numerous people to obferve the ceremonies above alluded to, from the first period of their inftitution to the prefent day, through a fucceffion of more than three thoufand years, with that uninterrupted and rigid adherence, with which the whole nation of the Jews have embraced them?

Examine the direct and immediate miracles of Mofes, from the time of croffing the Red Sea to the approach of the people to the promifed land, the principal of which are recapitulated by him in the 11th chapter of Deuteronomy, according to the criteria above laid down: and you will find in them every intrinfic mark of genuine truth and authenticity. They were fenfible effects, exceeding the known powers

powers of human nature : they were Sermon
ſo plain that every ſenſe was convinced VI.
of them ; and as public, as the preſence
of multitudes could render them. They
were inſtantaneous and compleat : and
the reſult of them was a notorious and
permanent effect. The internal character of divine power, diſplayed in the
performance of them, is marked by the
doctrine, which they tended to eſtabliſh ;
the doctrine of pure Theiſm : and the
effect, that hath been already experienced from them, is the acknowledgment of that doctrine by the much
greater part of the globe.

What then do we collect from the
preceding obſervations, reſpecting the nature and extent of the religion of the
Jews? Briefly this : that it is founded
in truth, imperfect in its inſtitution, ex-
tenſive in its influence. It was not a religion, conſiſting of fopperies borrowed
from different nations, framed by different
perſons, and put together at different
M times,

times, one fuperadded to another. It was the ftupendous work of one man: by him propofed to a numerous people; from the moment it was propofed, by that people univerfally received; and to the prefent period of time uninterruptedly obferved. The purity of it was guarded with uncommon caution : for fear of introducing corruptions into it, the interefts of policy were difregarded, and national advantages overlooked; the people were reftricted from intermarriages with other nations, and thereby precluded from ftrengthening themfelves by thofe advantageous alliances, which from fuch ties are often derived. A numerous and refpectable priefthood was inftituted and fupported : their fole charge the confervation of the pure religion committed to them; the employment of their lives the duties and fervice of it. It involved their whole law, and by the priefts was read and expounded to the people every week. And does not all this form, and care, and ceremony; this fo expedite

pro-

promulgation, so ready and general acceptance of it, even had it wanted those genuine characters of divinity, which miracles stamped on it, mark its preeminence to every other religion of the world; and demonstrate its truth?

But with all those characters of divinity and truth, it was imperfect. Its rites and ceremonies discovered nothing intrinsically wise and good: they were plain allusions to something that was to succeed. And even its moral part, though far as it went compleat, was destined to receive improvement. It was very indecisive in its doctrine of a future state: its promises were national, temporal; as to period of time uncertain, and probably distant. To some future period they were taught to direct their views: and thither they looked, as for the completion of their greatness, so likewise for the perfection of their knowledge. They wanted direct and satisfactory information on many points: left by the providence

dence of God, on many important articles, involved in a degree of darknefs; in order to add luftre to the advent of that eminent perfonage, they were taught to expect, the Meffiah; who, when he came, *would teach them all things.*

As to the influence of this religion, whether regarding time or place, fo extenfive was it; that it was deftined to reach from pole to pole, and to continue to the end of the world. All nations were comprehended in its promifes; and the gradual performance of them, proceeding with time, was ordained to be completed and perfected in immortality.

This religion, in its rites and ceremonies, in whatever parts of it were prefigurative and typical, is now a dead religion; no longer engaging the attention of mankind, or claiming their obfervance of it. But its moral parts, far as its doctrines go, are unchangeably good.

good. Let us therefore confider it as a valuable relic : let us regard it with that reverence, it merits : a light, firft fhining in an obfcure place, but from the time, when it was given, increafing in brightnefs more and more ; and in its deftined period breaking out in meridian luftre : its rays ftill continuing to diverge ; until its *light fhall lighten the Gentiles*, and all the world fhall acknowledge THE GLORY OF ISRAEL.

SERMON VII.

Matt. xxii. 42.

What think ye of Chrift ?

SERMON VII.

IN the great concern of inftructing mankind in the knowledge of God, and the duties from thence refulting, we have feen how far the powers of reafon went: its incompetence to that effect hath been proved from fact and experience; and the confequent neceffity of a revelation inferred. From that inference, without defcending to a comparative view of fuch revelations, as have refpectively urged their claim to divinity; which, with great judgment and erudition, hath, on the occafion that now engages my attention, been already done; *

* See White's Sermons.

I pro-

I proceeded to examine the merits of that revelation, which hath the moſt undoubted pretenſions to it: and, I truſt, ſatisfactorily evinced, that the revelation made to the Jews, though in the firſt period of its promulgation reſtricted to a ſingle nation, was deſtined in its iſſue to become univerſal: and even in the mean time, amidſt the viciſſitudes of that people, in their migrations from one country to another, whether in a ſtate of conqueſt or captivity, they left ſcattered remnants of the truths committed to them wherever they went. And hence have thoſe adumbrations of antient facts, which may be traced in prophane hiſtory, embelliſhed by poetic imagination, contributed not a little to the various ſyſtems of Heathen mythology. Even the expectation of a Meſſiah extended farther, than the religion of the Jews: towards the period of Chriſt's appearance in the world, the attention of the Heathen was in ſome degree excited to the advent of an illuſtrious character,

racter, who should form the world to happiness; teaching them all things that it was expedient to know, and performing all that was necessary to be done, in order to promote universal bliss, and effectuate the prosperity of mankind.

And as this general expectation of the Jews, declared by a series of prophecy, supported the truth of that Messiah's appearance, when Christ came, and in that character professed himself; no exertions have been spared, to invalidate the force of such expectations. It hath been asserted, that it was very natural for people under oppression to look forward, and flatter themselves with the hopes of some great character; who should rise up among them, and break their servile yoke: — that the Jewish priests by their enigmatical oracular declarations cherished those expectations in the people, in order to quicken their exertions; — and that the Jews were a credulous, enthusiastic people, always open

open to the deceptions of the crafty prieſthood.

SERMON VII.

In my preſent diſcourſe, therefore, I propoſe, 1ſt, to conſider the general expectation of a Meſſiah, that prevailed amongſt the Jews; and in this diſcuſſion to examine diſtinctly the objections to it, as already ſtated.

And to enquire, 2dly, whether their prophets repreſent him to have been a temporal prince and conqueror, or ſomething greater.

I. The firſt of theſe points, it is obvious, regards thoſe, who deny the truth of revelation; and who, to invalidate the doctrine of a promiſed Meſſiah, a doctrine on which the Chriſtian religion reſts, deſcribe the Jews as a credulous, enthuſiaſtic people, oppreſſed by their conquerors, impatient under their ſufferings, and taught by former deliverances, often great and unexpected, *ſo much be-*
yond

yond all that they hoped for, to look forward to some future Moses, Joshua, or Zerubbabel; the deliverer a fictitious character, and the doctrine a delusion of priestcraft and imposture.

If only when smarting under the oppressive arm of conquest, in their forlorn migrations, or in their various scenes of captivity, those prophetic declarations of a future deliverer had been pronounced; there might have been some degree of pertinency in the reflection, that attributes them to delusive expectations, derived from desperation and distress. But in the most flourishing and prosperous state of the nation, during their most brilliant periods of conquest and success, regularly and uniformly did their prophets predict the advent of an illustrious person of their own nation; destined to *establish a kingdom that should endure for ever.* Even the most successful and powerful princes themselves, in the spirit of prophecy, declared the time would come;

come; when under a powerful prince, whom the Lord would send to visit Israel, *all nations should be gathered under God:* that he would then *set up a kingdom, which should never be destroyed; and all that should see them,* when the kingdom of their Messiah should be established, *shall acknowledge them, that they are a seed blessed of the Lord.* In short, the whole tenour of the Old Testament points out, and the great scope of it seems particularly directed to, that first and great purpose, the establishment of a belief in one particular person, destined to *reign and prosper; and execute judgment and justice on the earth:* whose title, importing his high office, was to be, THE LORD OUR RIGHTEOUSNESS: who was to possess *dominion, and glory, and a kingdom,* so universal; that *all people, nations, and languages should serve him.* His dominion is described as *an everlasting dominion, which should not pass away; and his kingdom that, which should not be destroyed.*

Nor

SERMON VII.

Nor was this notion entirely confined to the Jews: Tacitus, in his account of that people, speaks of it as an expectation entertained by many; but refers the foundation of it to certain doctrines contained in the scriptures of their priests. "Pluribus persuasio inerat, antiquis sacerdotum litteris contineri, eo ipso tempore fore, ut valesceret Oriens, profectique Judæa rerum potirentur: quæ ambages Vespasianum et Titum prædixerant."* †

Josephus has the same observation: and imputes to the influence of such prediction the vigorous exertions of the Jews, in the course of that fatal war, which ended in the desolation of their city. "Το δε επαραν αυτας μαλιστα προς τον

* Tacitus Hist. lib. v.
† A general persuasion prevailed, that in the antient scriptures of their priests it was declared; the power of the East should be established, and from Judæa those should proceed, who would obtain the sovereignty of the world: which mysterious prediction was fulfilled in Vespasian and Titus.

" πολεμον,

"πολεμον, ην χρισμος αμφιβολος ομοιως εν τοις
"ιεροις ευρημενος γραμμασιν, ως κατα τον καιρον
"εκεινον, απο της χωρας τις αυτων αρξει της οικου-
"μενης. Τουτο οι μεν ως οικειον εξελαβον, και πολ-
"λοι των σοφων επλανηθησαν περι την κρισιν.
"Εδηλα δ'αμα την περι Ουεσπασιανα το λογιον ηγε-
"μονιαν, αποδειχθεντος επι Ιουδειας αυτοκρα-
"τορος." * †

SERMON VII.

Cicero, in a letter to Lentulus, alludes to a Sibylline oracle, purporting the fame event; which he applies to Ptolomy. "Cum eam [nempe Alexandriam] "pace præfidiifque firmaris, Ptolomæus "redeat in regnum; ita fore, ut per te

* Joseph. lib. vi. cap. xxxi.
† But what chiefly excited their exertions, and supported their perseverance in the war, was an equivocal oracle, which appears to have been found in their antient scriptures; purporting, that about that time some one from that country should sway the sceptre of the world, And the person, so designed, they understood to be one of their own nation: a circumstance, in which many of their most learned were deceived. For it is very clear, that the prediction referred to the sovereignty of Judæa possessed by Vespasian.

" resti-

SERMON VII.
"reſtituatur, quemadmodum ſenatus
"iniçio cenſuit : et ſine multitudine re-
"ducatur, quemadmodum homines re-
"ligioſi Sibyllæ placere dixerunt." * †

Nor will the pretended character of the Jews, as being a credulous and enthuſiaſtic people, add any weight to the preceding objection; founded on the feelings of deſperation and diſtreſs. Enthuſiaſm and credulity might have prompted them to take up arms, and lift under the banner of every adventurous chief, who ſhould have ambition or addreſs ſufficient to ſet himſelf up for that *Son of Promiſe*. It is the nature of enthuſiaſm and credulity, to prompt to raſh and daring enterpriſes. They allow no

* Cic. lib. 1. Epiſt ad Lent.
† When you have effected the peace ſtabliſhment of Alexandria, and properly garriſoned it. Let Ptolomy return to his kingdom : ſo will he appear to be reſtored by you, as the ſenate at firſt determined; and to be brought back without tumult or violence, as religious men have ſuppoſed the Sibyl predicted.

time

time to reafon and reflect: they warm Sermon
the heart with a fort of hallowed fire; VII.
that impetuoufly preffes forward with a
power fuperiour to the love of glory,
and vanquifhes doubt by a principle
more efficacious than the dread of fhame.
Actuated only by the goad of defpera-
tion, and the influence of enthufiafm
and credulity, the Jews would not fo
paffively have borne their hopes and expectations for fo many ages, as they
were known to have done: their prophets in a long fucceffion continuing to
promife them a Meffiah, and they in
full conviction of the truth of fuch promifes patiently continuing age after age
to expect him.

Nor do the accounts, with which the
annals of that people furnifh us, of a
banditti of profligate and diforderly men,
affembled under the conduct of this or
that defperate chief, who might boaft
himfelf of confequence, and affume the
character of a deliverer, affect the truth
of

Sermon VII.

of the above remark. No ſtate is free from partial inſurrections of men ruined and deſperate; who frame grievances, and oppoſe order, for the ſake of rapine and plunder. Thoſe riotous mobs do not invalidate the argument, againſt the imputation of enthuſiaſm, credulity, and deſperation; founded on the quiet, paſſive, general expectation of a Meſſiah: by their prophets deſcribed in characters very different from thoſe, which mark the ruffian leaders, that in the Jewiſh, as well as every other ſtate, may have occaſionally drawn together a rabble for purpoſes ſuch as theſe. Or, if independent of every motive of licentiouſneſs and rapine, the bare pretence of Meſſiahſhip had power and influence enough to draw together a company of men, ready at the hazard of their lives to ſupport ſuch an expectation; the effect evinces the ſtrong and efficacious perſuaſion of the real advent of a promiſed Meſſiah.

And

And as to the pretence of such promises having been the forgery of their priests, calculated to call forth the exertions of the people under any enterprising chief that might occasionally arise, of courage to attempt, and conduct to execute, a plan of deliverance from captivity or bondage, and establish once more their kingdom by conquest; those prophecies, to afford any ground for the supposition, must have been confined to the day of tribulation: which has been already observed not to be the case. Their priests also in the commission of such acts of forgery, their priests must have been wretched politicians; a reflection this, which does not appear founded in exact truth; and their chiefs and civil officers very negligent and remiss, in suffering such incentives to anarchy and confusion to be proposed to the people. We must therefore conclude, that the predictions in the old testament of a Messiah, the prophecies of kings and princes, declared in times of prosperity, as well as in periods of distress, regular-

Sermon VII.

ly continued in a courfe of near two thoufand years, were not the forgeries of priefts: and, that the people's belief in them, was not the effect of enthufiafm and credulity, but a rational affent; an affent, which neither the varying circumftance of affluence or penury could alter, the falfe pretenfions of perfons, who had at different times affumed that character, could remove, nor difappointment of any kind induce them to relinquifh. For what is it, that could effect this, but a rational ground of belief; what is it, that could render fuch a notion fo efficacious and univerfal, but the genuine ftamp of divinity and truth?

If however we be to have it eternally in our ears, that the Jews are an enthufiaftic and credulous people: without allufion to the confequences, let us freely examine the objection itfelf; and it will be found to a degree futile and abfurd. An individual or two may be credulous and enthufiaftic. A whole family, through

through some successions, held in ignorance, and biassed by the early prejudice of parental example, may possess minds strongly tinctured with enthusiasm and credulity. It shall even be allowed that a whole nation, while they continue immersed in barbarism, and involved in ignorance, may from those circumstances derive an enthusiastic zeal and bigotry in support of false tenets, which they may have credulously adopted. But that nature should as it were have moulded the minds of a whole nation with a peculiar disposition to believe absurd, and fancy vain, things; a nation, who have lived, at various periods, among the most polished and scientific people of the world; who among themselves have boasted many characters eminent for their great erudition; who have with freedom canvassed, and with abilities investigated, the volume, that contains their own religion; have, in their admission of the contents of that volume, discriminated truth from falshood, facts from pretences, records of authenticity from

Sermon VII. from doubtful relations; and, what may weigh moſt with the characters, to whom theſe reflections are particularly addreſſed, a liberal-minded people, who had their free-thinkers, as well as we: that credulity and enthuſiaſm ſhould be the conſtitutional characteriſtics of ſuch a people, is a paradox, which ſober reaſon can never explain. But any thing it ſeems is to be admitted, rather than a doctrine tending to ſupport the credibility of a religion, whoſe univerſality levels the diſtinction of illiterate and wiſe; whoſe large pale, exalting virtue whereever found, comprehends every good heart, and willing mind: humiliating to philoſophic pride; and at the ſame time ſo inconſiſtent with the purſuits of the voluptuous, that they muſt either renounce their pleaſures, or give up all the advantages their religion propoſes.

Having thus endeavoured to obviate the objections, that have been advanced againſt the doctrine of a promiſed Meſſiah;

siah; it would be a vain intrusion on your time, farther to particularise the scriptural predictions importing such a promise, or more at large to infist on proofs of the universal credit, the Jews themselves gave to the doctrine; looking forwards to the destined period with animated hopes. It is a doctrine by their prophets so plainly revealed, and so earnestly enforced; that if, deaf to the voice of prophecy, blind to the appeal of miracles, without one good reason for so perverse a conduct, the Jews had rejected it; deservedly would they have incurred the reproach of the most invincible stupidity, that ever marked a devoted people. It was uninterruptedly inculcated by all their prophets, down from Moses to Malachi: who uniformly predicted a particular kingdom, that God would erect, which should never be destroyed; and a particular person, whose dominion was to be an everlasting dominion. ONE particular king, and not a race of kings, is throughout the whole line of prophecy defigned. The Jews underftood it fo; and from fuch interpretation of the predictions concluded, that the Meffiah fhould never die. Accordingly when our Saviour gave intimation of his death: the Jews immediately replied, *we have heard out of the law, that Chrift abideth for ever; how fayeft thou then, that the fon of man muft be lifted up?* And when he talked to his difciples of his death and fufferings; Peter could not bear a reflection that fo fhocked his hopes, and anfwered, *that be far from thee, Lord.*

And after prophecy was filent; that is, from the time of Malachi to the advent of our Lord, the expectation of Ifrael did not ceafe. Indeed, as the time deftined for the completion of this important prophecy approached; the hope of the promife became more and more lively. Some of the heathen oracles caught the ray of illumination: and about the time, that our Saviour vifited the

the world, the expected appearance of a great and powerful prince became fo common; that it was applied, as hath been already intimated, to feveral heathen princes. And from that fo general and prevalent expectation, fome have attacked the doctrine on the ground of its novelty: as a notion, which firft obtained credit about the time of Herod.

But, fays Voffius, we muft go farther back for it: fo far as the time, when Pompey made himfelf mafter of Jerufalem: fifty nine years before Chrift, and exactly on the completion of Daniel's fixty fecond week.* Suetonius fpeaks of a prediction, previous to the birth of Auguftus; " Regem Populo Romano " naturam parturire." † And Cicero alludes to the fame oracle, as well in the epiftle to Lentulus cited above, as in the following paffage in his treatife on

---
* Voffius de fibyllinis oraculis lib. iv.

† That nature was in labour of a king deftined to rule the Romans.

Sermon VII.

divination. * " Sibyllæ verfus obferva-
" mus, quos illa furens fudiffe dicitur.
" Quorum interpres nuper falfa quædam
" hominum fama dicturus in Senatu
" putabatur: cum, quem revera regem
" habebamus, appellandum quoque effe
" regem, fi falvi effe vellemus." † This
oracle was applied to Julius Cæfar: on
which interpretation Cicero, glowing
with the flame of patriotifm, proceeds;
" Cum antiftitibus agamus, et quidvis
" potius ex illis libris, quam regem
" proferant : quem Romæ pofthæc nec
" dii, nec homines effe patientur."‡
After the death of Cæfar, this illuftrious

* Lic. de divinitatione lib. ii.

† Obferve the verfes of the Sibyl, which the frantic prieftefs is faid to have dictated : whofe interpreter was thought to have drawn from thence in the fenate falfe conclufions; fuggefting, that he, whom we in reality admitted as king, muft be acknowledged and ftiled a king, if we wifh to be faved.

‡ But might I exchange a word with the priefts, I would recommend it to them, rather to produce any thing from their books, than a king: whom neither Gods or men will ever fuffer hereafter to exift in Rome.

prophecy

prophecy was applied to Auguftus: Virgil compliments his friend and patron Pollio with the application of it to his infant fon: and others again fubfcribed to the grofs adulation of Jofephus; who condefcended to betray the high privileges of his nation, and applied the promife to Vefpafian. Many extracts might be made from the Sibylline books, alluding to different circumftances attending that promifed event; but I will content myfelf with producing the fingle one, adverted to by the authors, whom I have cited above.

Αυταρ επει Ρωμη τε και Αιγυπτɤ Βασιλεια
Εις εν διθυνɤσα, τοτε δη Βασιλεια μεγιςη
Αθανατɤ Βασιλνος επ' ανθρωποισι φανειται *
Ηξει δ' αγνος αναξ πασης γης σκηπτρα κρατησων
Εις αιωνας παντας επειγομενοιο χρονοιο.
Και τοτε Λατινων απαραιτητος χολος ανδρων,
Τρεις Ρωμην οικτρη μοιρη καταδηλησονται.*

From

* Orac. Sibyl. lib. ii.
But after Rome and Egypt fhall unite

Their

SERMON VII.

From what has been above obferved, it is beyond contradiction evident; that the doctrine of a promifed Meffiah is not only afferted in the fcriptures of the Old Teftament, but by heathen oracles declared; not only believed by the Jews, but admitted and adverted to by profane authors, of the firft rank, and the moft polifhed ages. Let us then proceed to the fecond article of enquiry: which was, whether the prophets reprefent the Meffiah as a temporal prince and conqueror, or fomething greater.

II. In fuppofing the Meffiah to appear in the character of a powerful and triumphant prince, who fhould eftablifh the kingdom of Ifrael on fo fure and

> Their powers, and an extended empire rife;
> A prince immortal fhall the fceptre fway:
> A king immaculate; whofe realms no line
> Shall circumfcribe, his reign no point of time.
> Inexorable then the rage of Rome:
> And under three the power of Rome fhall fall.

folid

solid a foundation, that it should through all ages continue miſtreſs of the world, and that all nations should finally ſubmit to it ; the Jews had one great difficulty to encounter : and this was the ſtate of humiliation, in which ſome prophecies repreſented him. An oppreſſed and de-ſpiſed Saviour, ſuffering inſults, and neither in word or act vindictively retaliating, diſplaying not the indignant ſpirit of an earthly conqueror, but an exemplar of meekneſs, patience, and humility, was little calculated to aſſume the port of worldly grandeur ; and, by the workings of a bold and daring mind, to keep a profligate world in awe : it confounded their expectations, and croſſed the proud and towering hopes, they had entertained of him.

A State of ſuch deſcription as this did by no means comport even with the flattering ideas, his own diſciples at firſt formed of his future greatneſs. Depreſſed and diſpirited at his crucifixion, they

SERMON VII.

SERMON VII.

they gave up every thing for loſt: and mourned their diſappointed hopes in their crucified maſter; whom they then deplored, that they had vainly *thought to have been him, who ſhould have redeemed Iſrael.* But this erroneous opinion we find ſoon corrected: for after he had *explained to them the ſcriptures concerning himſelf*; they, who on his apprehenſion had denied, and on his crucifixion had loſt all hopes in him, after his reſurrection and their frequent converſations with him, ſtood boldly forth in his defence: publickly arraigned the Jews for their impiety in having murthered an innocent perſon, and Him their own Meſſiah, the Lord of life; and gloried in ſuffering ignominy and ſtripes for his ſake. So clearly did thoſe ſcriptures, properly underſtood, point out a ſuffering Saviour.

This ſuffering ſtate of the Meſſiah, deſcribed in terms ſo explicit, as ſome thought could not be denied, and ſo glaringly

glaringly contradicting the idea of that Sermon
glorious state, in which all expected VII.
their Messiah to appear, raised a difficulty; which to obviate, two methods
have by the later Jews been devised : one
explaining it away, and the other deny-
ing the application of it.

1. First, in evasion of those prophecies,
so injurious as the Jews conceived them
to the dignity of their Saviour and Deliverer; the doctrine of the supposed
advent of two different Messiahs was
adopted : the one an afflicted, suffering
Messiah, destined to teach them patience
and resignation ; and the other a great
and glorious prince, sent to reward them
for their sufferings. But this notion has
not the least foundation in the scriptures : where the Messiah is constantly,
uniformly, and clearly represented, as
the one Redeemer, *the Holy One of Israel :
the Lord said unto my Lord, thou art a
priest for ever* : and the like. It is a
futile and vain conceit, without any authority

SERMON VII.

thority from their moſt antient and genuine writings to ſupport it. And they may with equal pretence admit a number of Meſſiahs, as two; Elijah, Jeremiah, and every afflicted ſuffering prophet, that was ſent to them. *

2. The other mode of interpretation denies the application of thoſe deſcriptions to the Meſſiah: referring them to their nation at large, as figurative repreſentations of it in its ſeveral periods of captivity and oppreſſion. But if the predictions of the glorious appearance of the Meſſiah be taken in a literal ſenſe; we have the ſame ground for applying a literal meaning to thoſe prophecies, that deſcribe his humiliation.

* Vid. Pocock Appen. ad. Comm. in Malachi: Ch. iii. V. 1. Ecce ego mitto angelum meum, et præparabit viam meam, et ſtatim veniet ad templum ſuum Dominus, quem vos quæritis, et Angelus Fæderis, quem vos vultis; ecce venit, dicit Dominus Exercituum.

Who of the Jews, antient or modern, ever doubted of the following reprefentations being defcriptive of the Meffiah? " Unto us a child is born, unto us a fon " is given: and the government fhall " be upon his fhoulders; and his name " fhall be called Wonderful, Counfel- " lor, the Mighty God, the Father " of the everlafting Age, the Prince of " Peace: of the increafe of his govern- " ment and peace there fhall be no end, " upon the throne of David, and upon " his kingdom to fix it, and to eftablifh " it, with judgment, and with juftice, " henceforth and for ever." Again: " The fpirit of the Lord fhall reft upon " him, the fpirit of wifdom and under- " ftanding, the fpirit of counfel and " ftrength; the fpirit of the knowledge " and fear of Jehovah: and he fhall be " of quick difcernment in the fear of " Jehovah, fo that not according to the " fight of his eyes fhall he judge, nor " according to the hearing of his ears " fhall he reprove; but with righteouf-
" nefs

SERMON VII.

SERMON VII.

"ness shall he judge the poor, and with "equity shall he work conviction on "the meek of the earth. He shall "smite the earth with the blast of his "mouth, and with the breath of his "lips shall he slay the wicked." Is there any one, that affixes to those descriptions of Isaiah a figurative meaning? Certainly not: and for this just reason; because the literal sense is plain and obvious, admitting no doubt, and involving no difficulty. There is nothing forced, or strained, or inconsistent in the literal meaning; and therefore every rule of sound criticism witholds us from flying to a figurative interpretation.

If by the same rule of criticism we judge the same prophet's representation of the humiliated state of the Messiah; we shall find it charactered in as strong lines in the 53d chapter of Isaiah, as his exalted state has been noted in the passages above adduced. Indeed this description, taken in a literal sense, is not only

only plain throughout, and uniformly perfpicuous : but in affixing a figurative meaning to it, and applying it to the Jewifh nation, there are parts of it, fuch as refer to the atonement of the Meffiah ; which are perfectly, irreconcileable with every accommodation of common fenfe. For inftance : " furely our infirmities " hath he borne; and our forrows, he " hath carried them : yet we thought " him judicially ftricken, fmitten of " God, and afflicted. But he was " wounded for our tranfgreffions : he " was fmitten for our iniquities. The " chaftifement, by which our peace is " effected, was laid upon him ; and by " his bruifes we are healed." Take this paffage figuratively : and I conceive it will be very difficult to prove the connection, the neceffary connection between the fuffering ftate of the Jewifh nation at one period, and its eafy, peaceful, happy ftate at another ; or by what nice and fecret train of caufes and effects

this

this depended on, and was effected by, the other.

What conclusion then do these reflections produce? Clearly this. That the absurd device of the later Jews to obviate the predictions of the humiliated state of the Messiah, by the admission of two Messiahs, tends to establish the belief of a suffering Messiah. And with regard to the other opinion of such description, as figurative of the Jewish nation; the letter is so irreconcileable with the figure, as to destroy every attempt at accommodation. And the inference from thence must be; that, those prophetic descriptions of the Messiah being in both instances literal, in him must meet the abasement of a meek, humble, oppressed, persecuted person, and the august glories of a prince, whose government and kingdom shall last for ever.

Full as the Jews were of the idea of a Saviour and Deliverer, a powerful and puissant

puissant prince, who should obtain for them universal empire; we are not surprised to find them endeavouring by every means, determined by any forced and foreign construction, to get rid of the doctrine of a suffering Messiah. But we have also seen, that the very same arguments, which prove his glorious and exalted state, are equally strong in evincing his humiliation. And obstinate as they have been in rejecting the declarations of their own prophets respecting the one; we will next enquire, whether their notions respecting the other be more consonant with their scriptures. Their opinion is briefly this:
" that an illustrious prince should rise
" up among them, and by force of
" arms establish his kingdom: that
" under his auspices they should tri-
" umph over their enemies, and that
" even to the latest period of time Jerusa-
" lem should give law to all the world."
With this opinion I proceed to confront some of those prophecies, which are

Sermon VII. unanimously considered as descriptive of the state and character of a glorious and exalted Messiah.

And first, had they well considered the whole scope of the prophecies relating to the kingdom of the Messiah; they would have been convinced that a spiritual, and not a temporal, kingdom was pourtrayed. *Righteousness and equity*, according to the prophecies already cited, are the constant marks of it; and not conquests charactered in blood: *with judgment and justice* it was to be supported; and not by the oppressive arm of strength: by *the knowledge and fear of Jehovah* it was to be maintained, and not by the rod of earthly power. *I the Lord*, saith Isaiah, *have called thee in righteousness, and will hold thine hand, and will keep thee; and give thee for a covenant of the people, for a light of the Gentiles, to open the blind eyes, and bring out the prisoners from the prison, and them, who sit in darkness, out of their prison house.* His office

office is here plainly defcribed to confift in the diffemination of true knowledge : he is marked out, or *called forth*, as it is expreffed, not by exploits of conqueft, but as an exemplar of righteoufnefs : his deftination is, not to controul the world with the authority of a chief and conqueror, but to diffeminate heavenly knowledge even among the Gentiles ; and by the illumination of the fpirit to open the underftanding of the blind, and releafe them from the prifon houfe of ignorance and fin. And how compleatly he fhould be qualified for thefe high offices another prophecy declares : *There shall come forth a rod out of the stem of Jesse, and a branch shall grow out of his root ; and the spirit of the Lord shall rest upon him, the spirit of wisdom and understanding, the spirit of counsel and might, the spirit of knowledge and piety, and the fear of the Lord.*

The text, I have next to produce, feems particularly addreffed to their prejudiced

SERMON
VII.

judiced opinion of a temporal prince and mighty conquerour. *He shall not cry*, or more properly, *shout*, which the original word יצעק׳ in this place fignifies, and under it the shout of war is alluded to, *nor lift up, nor cause his voice to be heard in the streets: a bruised reed shall he not break, nor quench the smoaking flax; but he shall bring forth judgment unto truth: he shall not be crushed, nor discouraged, till he hath set judgment in the earth, and the Gentiles shall* BELIEVE IN HIS NAME. This prophecy is not only defcriptive of what the Meffiah fhould be, but declarative of what he fhould not be. It declares that his appearance fhall not be in the character of a warrior; an invader of territories, to which he has no right, and a ftormer of peaceful cities: but that fo inoffenfive fhould he appear, fo far from exertions of power, fo far from leading war and deftruction in his train; that he fhould not even break a bruifed reed, fhould exercife no act of violence, nor carry defolation into the moft impotent ftate; implied under the figure of extinguifhing

guifhing the feeble light of an expiring SERMON
lamp. The object of atchievement, to VII.
which he was deftined, was not to render the Gentiles tributary to Jerufalem,
but to bring the Gentiles into a common
hope in Jerufalem's Meffiah ; to conciliate a BELIEF in his name, a truft and
confidence in the divinity of his miffion.

If we examine the 45th pfalm, which
the Jewifh doctors unanimoufly acknowledged to be prophetic of the Meffiah,
notwithftanding the figures of worldly
majefty under which he is defcribed, it
is plainly declared that He fhall profper
and reign BECAUSE *of his truth, and meek-
nefs, and righteoufnefs* ; *that his throne
fhould be for ever and ever* : and, as a
characteriftic of his kingdom, that *the
fceptre of it fhould be a fceptre of* RIGHTE-
OUSNESS. The 110th pfalm has the fame
general evidence of the learned Jews,
in proof of its reference to the Meffiah.
He is there reprefented, as an everlafting
high prieft : a term fignificant of his
holinefs:

SERMON VII.

holiness: and termed by David, *his Lord*; who should sit at the right hand of God, there to contemplate the subjugation of his enemies. Doth this description comport with the character of an earthly conqueror? And doth it not comport with that of a heavenly delegate? And as the nature of heavenly greatness is indescribable by an earthly pen, it was natural to cloath it under images of mortal glory. And what scene of earthly glory equals that of triumphant power and conquest? *The Lord shall send the rod of thy strength out of Zion; rule thou in the midst of thine enemies. The Lord at thy right hand shall strike through kings in the day of his wrath: He shall fill the places with the dead bodies: He shall wound the heads over many countries.*

Let us next examine the prophecy of Nathan; the former part of which directly points to Solomon: *he shall build me a house, and I will establish his throne for ever.* The prophet then, in the spirit

rit of divination, inftead of dwelling on his fubject, rapt with divine enthufiafm at the profpect prefented to his mind, directs his prediction to the endlefs duration of that kingdom under the Meffiah : declaring that God *would be His father, and He fhould be His fon: that He would fettle him in his houfe and in his kingdom for ever.* Good kings, and prophets, God fometimes denominates his fervants. So was Mofes ftiled, and David. But no one, except Chrift, was ever ftiled in an efpecial and particular manner His fon. The term FATHER, had it ftood alone, might perhaps have by fome been fuppofed to denote the tendernefs and affection, which God promifed to fhew him : but the antithetic term SON difcovers a more marked and reftricted meaning. It was too diftinguifhing a title, to be conferred on a mere human prince and governor. It was never applied to either of the characters noticed above ; and could with much lefs propriety be afcribed to an inferior one, as was Solomon :

mon: inferior in piety, in zeal for God, and concern for his people. Moses was a prince and leader, and David a king: both of them delegated by God for high purposes, and both of them prophets. Yet thus distinguished, they were never stiled the sons of God. SON OF GOD, was the reserved appellation of a superior character: but what character could be superior to both these, but something supra-human or divine? That other expression, *I will settle him* IN MY HOUSE, seems to bear an allusion to that particular holiness of character, which should distinguish the Messiah: and which, in the preceding quotation, was noted by the office of an everlasting priesthood.

Behold, saith Isaiah, the prophet from whom I have extracted most of the preceding quotations, and whose predictions, though confessedly delivered seven or eight hundred years before the appearance of Christ, are more like a history

tory of his life, than a prophecy; *behold, a king shall reign in righteousness, and princes,* that is princes under him, his ministers, *shall rule in judgment.* Jeremiah in still stronger colours characterises the Messiah: *and this is his name, saith he, whereby he shall be called,* THE LORD OUR RIGHTEOUSNESS. The word is, Jehovah our righteousness: He, in whose exalted merits shall be our righteousness; He, in whom we look for salvation: a salvation not placed in his conquests, in his military prowess and exploits of valour, but in his righteousness, holiness, equity, in all those virtues calculated to raise the mind, and fit it for universal bliss and endless happiness.

And is this the character, destined by a series of martial exploits to obtain the sovereignty of the world; and by His prowess hold that subject world in awe? Are those the means calculated to establish an universal monachy; and to crush the vigorous exertions of rival and contending

tending powers? Let the nation of Israel queſtion itſelf; whether holineſs, righteouſneſs, equity, and judgment, were the means, by which it eſtabliſhed even its narrow dominion in Paleſtine. Aſk them whether they did not wade through blood, through havock, and devaſtation, to that eſtabliſhment; which they effected, under their puiſſant heaven-favoured chiefs and princes, Moſes, Joſhua, David, and others. The object, the important object, we acknowledge, juſtified every ſtep they took: an object, of all that can concern mankind, the greateſt: the conſervation of the knowledge of God; and, from thence derived, a ſenſe of the love we owe Him, of the reverence with which we ought to regard Him, of the ſervice we are bound to pay Him.

Let them diſpaſſionately ſearch their own ſcriptures, and enquire whether they do not uniformly repreſent the dominion of the Meſſiah, as founded, and conſiſting

consisting in righteousness: whether they do not character His glory, in a stile superior to that of earthly grandeur; His *kingdom, as not of this world.* It may indeed appear strange, that those, who should seem most interested in what their prophets had declared, and whom one might conceive possessed of the greatest helps to understand them; that those, to whom the glad tidings were first sent, should stop their ears against them. But giving something to prejudice, and much to self-interest, for they had learned to expect present honour and advantage, we may in some measure account for that obstinacy; which shut up their hearts against every impression of truth. And when we hear their own prophets, in words inspired by God himself, declaring; *hear ye indeed, but understand not; and see ye indeed, but perceive not: the heart of this people is fat, and their ears heavy, and they shut their eyes; lest they should see with their eyes, and hear with their ears, and understand with their heart,*

and

Sermon VII.

SERMON *and convert and be healed:* the effect is
VII. explained; and their predicted miftake
of the Meffiah affords an additional argument to us, of the truth of His miffion: which fo pointedly meets the defcription of their prophets; and with the added particular of their own rejection of Him.

From the preceding reflections I will offer only one fhort inference, the inference of the great Apoftle to the Gentiles, drawn from fimilar reafoning: *wherefore if God fpared not the natural branches, take heed left He fpare not thee.* If the Jews, with eyes fo blinded, and hearts hardened againft the voice of truth, victims to invincible obftinacy, and inveterate prejudices, experienced fuch a feries of evils, as in no other national inftance ever marked a devoted people: let us profit by their example; and not by a fimilar conduct draw down upon ourfelves fimilar, or greater, evils: let us not, through love of pleafure and diffipation,

pation, neglect to know and to understand the sacred records of our religion; nor through vanity, and the little catchings at admiration, by daring to do, what really wife, and truly good men, would not do, affect to treat them with scorn. Let not the contemptuous air of irony and ridicule, nor any other motive whatever, divert us from studying, and from professing to study those volumes; on which a Newton, a Locke, and a Boyle were not ashamed to employ their great abilities, and valuable time. If any learning be worth pursuing; it is that, on which the interests of another world depend. *Search the scriptures; for in them are the words of eternal life.* And the farther we search them, of this truth we shall be the more convinced; and conviction will add new incitement to our labours: and the more we study, and the better we understand, the more we shall learn to value, them.

SERMON VIII.

Matt. xxii. 42.

What think ye of Christ?

SERMON VIII. UNDER this general subject, the questions discussed in my last discourse were, first whether the general expectation of a Messiah was founded in reason and truth : and secondly, whether that Son of Promise, destined to visit and redeem Israel, was to be a mere mortal, an illustrious prince and conquerour, or something greater ; of nature supra-human, and divine. And in this latter investigation I referred to the prophecies of the old Testament; which the Jews were found most wretchedly to have mistaken, and misrepresented : and, in
consequence

consequence of such misinterpretations, to have rejected a saviour, and with silly expectation looked forward to a conqueror. Misjudging nation! Was it for this, that Jehovah led you forth from the land of affliction ; and by a train of splendid miracles conducted you through the pathless sea, and waste wilderness, to your promised inheritance ? Was it for this the light of prophecy shone forth ; beaming blessings on mankind, and proclaiming a new æra of happiness to the world ? Had those prophecies no farther aspect, than to conquest and extended dominion ; to private ambition and public injury ? Wretched politicians ! Or ye would have known ; a warlike prince, such as your narrow prejudices figured your Messiah, though conquest like a slave seem chained to his triumphal car, is the greatest scourge an oppressed nation can experience. Did increased extent of public territory ever produce an increase of private happiness : or is it not notoriously otherwise ? Be that as it may:

Sermon VIII.

may: the Jews in general entertained no other idea of their Meſſiah, than that which worldly ſplendor ſuggeſted; the range of greatneſs and power.

And there is a ſect of Chriſtians alſo, that hold doctrines much the ſame: if indeed thoſe are to be called Chriſtians, who regard Chriſt with ſcarcely more reverence, than even the Mahometans themſelves; who deny to him every character of divinity, and every degree of diſtinction, above Peter, James, and the reſt of his followers, except that of maſter and diſciple. " It is evident, ' ſay they,' that the Jews themſelves " expected nothing more than a mere " man for their Meſſiah." And then is commonly cited in proof of it this prophecy of Moſes: *a prophet ſhall the Lord your God raiſe up unto you from among your brethren*, LIKE UNTO ME. And this likeneſs they conclude to conſiſt in dignity of character, rank, and nature: whereas the expreſſion alludes to

the

the office only; and the true and literal Sermon tranflation of the original is, "a pro- VIII. phet not like unto me, but as I am ως εμε, one who fhall fuftain the prophetic office, as I do, *fhall the Lord God raife up unto you, from among your brethren.* And if inftead of a loofe tranflation, the original had been confulted; it would have precluded fuch ground of Socinian cavil.

With regard to the general affertion, that " the Jews expected nothing more " than a mere man for their Meffiah;" it is very readily acknowledged: and the conclufion follows; that as they were charged by their own prophets, with having miftaken the fcriptures; and that charge was renewed againft them by our Saviour; their opinion is no proof of the truth of the doctrine they entertained. On the other hand,

* See Prieftley on the Influence of Philofophy on Chriftianity, p. 310.

SERMON VIII.

if it appear from the scriptures of the new Testament, that Christ is there represented as something more than mere man; the contrary opinion of the Jews tends to confirm the apparent doctrine of the new Testament, and to fulfil the prophecies of the old. To this investigation, then let us now proceed, and enquire into the nature and character of Messiah the Christ, as the scriptures of the new Testament represent him; with one previous observation: which is, that some line is to be drawn, according to which we must admit, or reject, figurative constructions. And the proper rule of admittance I conceive to be, when the literal one implies a contradiction to reason; or to other clear, direct, and positive texts of scripture. For if, as fancy prevails, figurative meanings be arbitrarily assigned; the doctrines of the new Testament could not be considered as a general rule of faith or practice: but must be liable, as whim and imagination

nation led, by every fanciful reader to be frittered away.

SERMON VIII.

The method, I propofe in the fequel to purfue, is; firft, to enquire what is the general fcope and tenor, which the fcriptures of the new Teftament, on the fubject of our prefent inveftigation purport and propofe: and fecondly, to meet the objections to Chrift's pre-exiftence and divinity, in the full force in which certain readers of a revived fect have preffed them.

I. To begin with the birth of Chrift, which the hiftories of the Evangelifts, Matthew and Luke, declare to have been in an eminent manner fupernatural, we find him introduced into the world without a human father; and therein charactered with a plain mark of individuation, which difcriminates him from all other men, and places him above the rank of human beings. *The Holy Ghoft fhall come upon thee, and the power of the highest*

SERMON VIII.

highest shall overshadow thee: therefore also that holy thing, διο και το γενωμενον αγιον, not Βρεφος, not that holy infant, child, or son; but that holy thing, or being, *which shall be born of thee, shall be called the Son of God.* Derived from a source thus divine, the production must necessarily partake of its divine origin: he was accordingly *called,* that is, he *was,* in a peculiar manner was, *the Son of God.* Look through nature, and observe if we have not as plain and powerful an argument in support of this doctrine, as analogy can afford. The Evangelist John also, in his account of the origin of Christ, as plainly as words can express a meaning, asserts his divinity, and also his pre-existence: declaring that he *was with God in the beginning*; and that by his instrumentality all things were made. This could not be affirmed of a mere man: and that this procemium of St. John's Gospel did refer to Christ,

it

it would lead me too far from my prefent Sermon
fubject to go about to prove.* VIII.

Agreeable to fuch divine origin is the next account we have of him, when the Holy Ghoft in a bodily form defcended on him ; and a voice from Heaven pronounced him to be the *beloved Son of God*. And uniformly and confiftently with the cœleftial declaration, when there is occafion to fpecify his nature, and teftify who he really is, he both ftiles himfelf, and is acknowledged by his difciples as, THE SON OF GOD. The condition addreffed to the Ethiopian eunuch, previous to his baptifm, was, *if thou believeft*. His anfwer evinces the extent of the implied queftion : *I believe that Jefus is the Son of God*. † Adam it is true was alfo ftiled the Son of God :

---

* See " Free Examination of the Socinian Expofition
" of the prefatory verfes of St. John's Gofpel."
Printed for W. Flexney.

† See Sermon I.

Sermon VIII.

becaufe God was his immediate author. But Chrift, notwithftanding Adam's priority in the flefh, is ftiled ὁ υἱος πρωτοτοκος. A diftinction this not without a difference, and the difference is plain: Adam was created by God, a mere human creature; and, being produced without father or mother, was therefore ftiled in the genealogical account of Chrift, the Son of God. But the difference of Chrift's procedure from God, is marked by the ftrong term τοκος, begotten: a term plainly expreffive of a communication of nature.

In the account of the tranfaction at the wedding at Cana, there is in the anfwer of our Lord to his mother fomething very declarative of a fuperiority of nature, above what appearances might challenge. *Woman*, not mother; *what concern have you with me?* What influence do you claim over me: to what dependence on you am I fubject? And much to the fame purpofe we find him continually

continually expressing himself, on any SERMON claims of earthly kindred. When, arguing with the doctors in the synagogue, it was told him; that his *mother and brethren stood without, desiring to speak with him*, he answered, *who is my mother; and who are my brethren? And stretching forth his hands to his disciples, he said; behold my mother, and my brethren!* The passage, connected with other reflections, that had at different times occasionally dropped from him, may in some such terms as the following be paraphrased. " Whatever appearances may speak me: " earthly connections have I none. I " am a stranger in this world; without " a home, or residence in it, where I " may lay my head; without one na- " tural relative, to engage me with the " tender tie of affection; without " other business here, than that which " I received in commission from above." Thus also on his mother's expostulation with him on another occasion; *thy father and I have sought thee sorrowing*: his answer

Sermon VIII. anfwer is fimilar and uniform. *Why is it, that ye fought me?* And then, indirectly declaring Jofeph not to be his father, he adds; *have ye not known,* are ye yet to learn, *that I muft be about* MY FATHER's *bufinefs*: that I am now acting in my proper fphere, that I am now about my real father's bufinefs, that I muft be employed as I am?

No mere man, no prophet ever affumed the power of forgiving fins: the forgivenefs of fins was univerfally held to be the prerogative of God alone; and therefore when our Lord exercifed that authority, the Scribes we find accufing him of blafphemy.* Hence then it follows, that arrogating to himfelf a power, which did not belong to man, he either affumed a greater authority than he had a right to exercife; or that he was fupra-human, and therefore took upon him no higher power than what ftrictly belonged to him.

* Matt. ix. 3.

When

When it is faid, Matt. xi. 27. that SERMON *no one knoweth the father, except the fon:* VIII. it is very clear, that the nature of the father is intended. And in the fame verfe when it is declared, that *no one knoweth the fon, but the father*; the context fhews, that the nature alfo of the fon is alluded to. For as to his office, many knew him to be the Meffiah; and acknowledged him as fuch. But the knowledge, here implied, appears to be of a very different and fuperior kind: a knowledge delivered immediately by the father; a knowledge, which man did not poffefs, for even his difciples do not appear to have been compleatly acquainted with it, till after his refurection; even the knowledge of his eternal power and godhead. *All things are delivered to me of my father: and no man knoweth the fon, but the father.*

After our Lord had filenced the Sadducees, on the fubject of a refurrection; the Pharifees we are told entered into
controverfy

SERMON VIII.

controversy with him: to whom He proposed the question in my text. They in reply returned him the usual answer: on which he pressed them with the prophetic declaration of David; *the Lord said unto* MY *Lord, sit thou on my right hand, until I make thy foes thy footstool.* And he then argues on the words with such force; that if he did not effect the conviction of his hearers, he at least left them without the power of reply. We might risk the issue of the present controversy on this single passage: so decisive is it in point. The scope of it appears too plain to be mistaken: I will therefore only enlarge on the words, and leave it to the most determined opponent of Christ's divinity, to find a different meaning.

Our Lord's general question was, " what think ye of the Messiah?"—
" We consider him, answer the Phari-
" sees, as an illustrious prince descended
" from that glorious king of Israel Da-
" vid."—

" And

"And nothing more, rejoins our Lord, than a great man, an illustrious prince?"—The reply is, "no." "If that were the case then, saith our Lord;" with what propriety could that great and glorious monarch, the greatest that ever filled the throne of Israel, in the spirit of prophecy declare of him, declare of any mere human being, however exalted in rank, or blazoned with victories, "that he was HIS Lord: and that Jehovah would seat him on his right hand?" Consider the just degree of profound reverence, with which the Jews contemplated Jehovah, whose adorable perfections no epithet will suit; whose name, except on the most solemn occasions, they feared to pronounce, and never heard it without a reverential bow: and the force of our Lord's argument applies with irresistible power; in demonstrating that the Messiah must be by nature superior to David, something more than man. And if we be asked what effect this argument

gument had on his hearers minds: the effect was such, as truth must ever produce on minds which obstinacy had feared with impenetrable callosity, the forced assent of silence. *They were not able to answer Him*: they could not refute his arguments; nor, without giving up their prejudices, and retracting their erroneous opinions concerning the nature of the Messiah, could they admit the force of them: they therefore made him no reply. *Nor durst any man from that day forth ask him any more questions.*

Of that day, and that hour, saith St. Mark, *knoweth no man; no, not the angels which are in heaven, neither the son, but the* FATHER. Though we may not presume to ground a doctrine on verbal construction, it may be alledged as a circumstantial evidence of the truth of it, when grounded on a firmer foundation: and as such I submit to consideration the preceding climax; which represents the nature of Christ, not only as distinct from,

and

and fuperior to that of mere man, but even above the angelic nature itfelf.

SERMON VIII.

The Evangelifts Matthew and Luke mention the circumftance, of John having fent two of his difciples to enquire of Jefus; whether he were that great prophet, John had been taught to expect, or not. Our Lord in anfwer refers them to his works; leaving their mafter from them to form his judgment of him. When they were gone, he very naturally addreffed to thofe, who were about him, fome reflections on the character of John: which He reprefented to have been fo high, that *among thofe who were born of woman there was not a greater prophet than he.* Then with allufion to his own nature, rank, and dignity, which the queftion afked by John's Difciples very aptly introduced, he added; *but he, that is leaft in the kingdom of heaven, is greater than he:* in the kingdom of heaven, in that kingdom, where previous to my exiftence

ence here on earth I enjoyed glory with my father, who is in heaven: great prophet as he is, of courſe he is very inferior to me. In ſupport of this expoſition I will only add, that the common gloſſes on the paſſage give no pertinency to the laſt clauſe; nor do they obviate an apparent falſity in the clauſe preceding: for if Chriſt had not conſidered himſelf, of a nature and dignity ſuperior to that of a mere prophet, he muſt at leaſt have excepted himſelf as a much greater prophet than John.

If from the evangelical hiſtories of Matthew, Mark, and Luke, we proceed to that of John; the ſcope and tenor of his goſpel we ſhall find ſtill more clearly declarative of the divinity and pre-exiſtence of Chriſt. To inculcate that doctrine, appears to have been the particular deſign of it. The prefatory verſes of that goſpel, as hath been already intimated, are full in point; and ſeem to have been directly levelled at the oppoſite error.

error. *In the beginning was the word, and the word was with God, and the word was God.* And, as if to enforce a doctrine that had by some been questioned, he repeats it: ουτος, this very word, *was in the beginning with God. All things were made by him, and without him was not any thing made, that was made. And the word was made flesh, and dwelt among us.* And this doctrine, adds the Evangelist, was confirmed by John the Baptist; who allowed him preference in honour, in consequence of such his priority of existence: *He was preferred above me, for he was before me.*

No man hath ascended up to heaven, but he that came down from heaven, even the Son of man which was in heaven. For the exposition of this verse, observe the context: for scripture is best explained by scripture. *Verily, verily, saith our Lord, we speak that we do know, and tes-*

John iii. 13.

SERMON VIII.

tify that we have seen; and ye receive not our witness. If I have told you earthly things, and ye believe not; how shall ye believe, if I tell you of heavenly things. No man ever ascended up to heaven, and there received in an enlarged mind the communication of divine knowledge: except him who came down from heaven, to whom alone that knowledge was communicated, even him, who had his first existence in heaven.* The force of this passage cannot be better ascertained, than by the figment fabricated by Socinus to elude it: who supposed Christ to have taken a journey to heaven after his baptism; and afterwards to have returned to the earth, and entered upon his ministry.

The Baptist in direct words testifies in acknowledgment of Christ's superiority, that *He came from above*: and then, as

* Ο ων εν τω ϒρανω. The participle present here, as in various other passages, has the signification of an imperfect.

it

it were in explanation of the term he had made ufe of, by the word ἀνωθεν *from above*, he inftructs his hearers, that he meaned *heaven*. *He, that cometh from above, is above all: he, that is of the earth, is earthly, and fpeaketh of the earth: He, that cometh from heaven, is above all.*

And in this declaration of our Lord, *I came down from heaven, not to do mine own will, but the will of Him that fent me*; he plainly affumes the doctrine of his having defcended from heaven, as a truth, to which that full affent, he had repeatedly demanded, he fuppofed was implicitly paid : and declares his motive for fuch an humiliation to have been obedience to his father's will; and his defign, a full determination in every article to purfue it. And in a few verfes diftant diftinguifhing himfelf, by the particular communication he had enjoyed with the father in heaven, as alone competent to know and teach the perfect will of God, he adds; *it is indeed written*

SERMON VIII.

written in the prophets, that all men shall be taught of God: not that any man hath seen the father, save he which is of God, he hath seen the father; he is intimately acquainted with the nature and essence of God, he alone exactly knows his will, and deep designs, his hidden counsels, secret, and unfathomable by the human mind.

This doctrine of Christ's divine nature and pre-existent state appears to have given offence to some of his followers: which however we find him very far from retracting, or explaining away. On the contrary, with an indignant reproof he adds, *does this offend you?* And then perseveringly maintaining the doctrine, he had clearly asserted, he foretels his future ascension to those mansions, he had formerly left: and asks them, if such an appeal to their senses would satisfy their doubts; *what and if ye shall see the Son of man ascend up, where he was before?*

His

His superiority of nature, in a chapter or two following, is in terms the most unequivocal again asserted: *ye are from beneath, I am from above; ye are of this world, I am not of this world:* and (as the chain of subsequent reasoning supplies) if you will not believe this account of myself, which I have so expressly and repeatedly declared; *ye shall die in your sins. Then said they unto him, who art thou?* To which question, expressive of the most invincible obstinacy on their part, he made them no other reply than, *the very same, that I said unto you from the beginning*, that I have constantly and uniformly declared myself; the Son of God, that came down from heaven to do my father's will, and redeem you from your sins: which great truth ye will not believe, and must therefore die in your sins. This passage evidently declares the reason, why they should die in their sins; because they did not believe him to be the Son of God, and to have come down from heaven, to do his father's

SERMON VIII. father's will, and to redeem them from their sins. And if their disbelief in that article was a sin; the doctrine, in which they were so urgently required to believe, was a truth.

Towards the close of the same chapter, we find the same doctrine again insisted on; and in terms so express, that his hearers, though they would not believe him, appear by their rude proceedings to have perfectly understood his meaning: for irritated at the claim of divinity, which he arrogated, *they took up stones to cast at him.* The offensive declaration was a direct assertion of his pre-existence: *before Abraham was, I am.*

In a conversation with his disciples, the plain scope of which was to prepare them for his departure, and console them under their loss, he tells them that in this world he counted not his origin, nor was the condition he had here assumed

his

his true and proper ftation; and that, in removing hence, he was only going to the place of exalted happinefs and glory, which in coming hither he had fo lately left. *I came forth from the Father, and am come into the world: again, I leave the world, and go to the father.* * The antithefes evince the literal meaning of the above paffage beyond a doubt. The world he was going to leave, was the very fame world into which he a little before had come; and the world, or ftate of exiftence, with the father, into which he was going to remove, was the world, or ftate of exiftence with the father, which, when he came to vifit this world, he had left. This the Difciples, to whom the words were particularly addrefled, underftood to be fo clear and intelligible; that they immediately obferved, *lo, now speakeft thou plainly, and speakeft no parable.*

---

* John xvi. 28.

SERMON VIII.

I will close this general examination of the histories of our Lord's life with a passage in that remarkable prayer, immediately preceding his apprehension; which throughout speaks the heart, and mind, and design, and interest of an inhabitant of another world, a stranger and sojourner here. *And now, O Father, glorify thou me with thine own self, with the glory which I had with thee before the world was.* These words plainly declare his pre-existence, and his pre-existence also in a state of glory; with the avowed consciousness of the glories of that his pre-existent condition. And as the generality of readers, I will say farther from the perspicuity of the passage, every impartial and unprejudiced reader, must so understand the import of the words: it follows, either that the declaration is calculated to deceive, or that it is absolutely true; either that Jesus arrogated in it a degree of pre-eminence, to which he had no claim, or

that

that he was of a nature supra-human, pre-existent, and divine.

After his resurrection he was constantly and uniformly preached by his apostles, as a superior being; not a separated soul in hades, nor a drowsy soul sleeping away a long period of existence in the grave: but as enjoying glory with God, that state of glory he had affirmed to have enjoyed with Him before his humiliation on earth. And the apostle Paul, in his Epistle to the Colossians, doth in the plainest language confirm the doctrine of his pre-existence; and, in that pre-existent state, of his instrumentality in the creation of the world *For in him were all things created, that are in heaven, and that are on earth, visible and invisible, whether they be thrones, or dominions, or principalities, or powers, all things were created through him and for him.* * And I the rather cite this pas-

---

* Col. i. 16. and 17.

SERMON VIII.

sage, as it forms a kind of comment; explaining, and confirming a similar assertion in St. John's Gospel in its primary and literal acceptation. *All things were made by him, and without him was not any thing made that was made.**

On these words of the Evangelist Socinus remarks, that " the words, *all
" things*, are not to be admitted in so
" general a sense as is commonly supposed, denoting the original formation
" of the world." — " They are not to
" be taken, ' continues he,' in their
" primary sense, as if referable to the
" material world; but are to be applied
" to the publication and reception of
" the gospel: as if John had said, all
" these spiritual and divine transactions,
" which are seen among us in the world,
" are derived from no other source than
" the preaching of the gospel of Jesus

* John i. 3.

" Christ;

"Chrift; and were effected by his in- Sermon
fluence and power." VIII.

That fuch interpretation of the words of the Evangelift is as falfe, as it is forced, foreign, and jejune, the preceding paffage cited from St. Paul demonftrates. It doth moft clearly afcertain the literal interpretation of the paffage in the Evangelift, and enforce the truth of it: evincing that the words could not be ufed in that figurative fenfe, Socinus hath affixed to them; nor referred to moral habits, and fpiritual improvements. Things *in heaven*, as well as *on earth*, *invifible*, as well as *vifible*, *whether they be thrones, dominions, principalities, or powers*, refer to a more extenfive creation, than that of new moral habits, a reformation of manners in this world; and difprove the idea of reftriction to this world, or any thing folely connected with it.

The general fcope and uniform tenor of the fcriptures of the new Teftament, refpecting

SERMON VII. respecting the doctrine of Christ's divinity and pre-existence, having thus endeavoured to evince; I proceed, as was proposed in the second place, to obviate some objections, that by certain writers of the present day have been advanced against it.

II. One objection to this doctrine is founded on the appellative man, in some passages of the new Testament applied to our Lord: as in Acts ii. 12. *Jesus of Nazareth, a man approved of God among you:* and again, *He hath appointed a day, in the which he will judge the world by that man, whom He hath ordained.* Acts, xvii. 31. And to these passages, from the Epistle of Paul to Timothy, I will add another; *there is one mediator between God and man, the man Christ Jesus:* remarking on this last passage, that the idea of a mere man being delegated to the high and important office of mediator between God and man, that is, between God and himself, is less agreeable

able to reason, than the doctrine of a superior and divine existence, by inheritance so claiming, or so ordained.

Respecting the general application of the denominative MAN to Christ, we know that the Evangelist John says, he *was made*, or became, *man:* and as such, he is in scripture frequently stiled MAN. But who is he, that St. John declares was made, or became, this individual man? Even that Divine Being, that existed with the father from the beginning. Acknowledging therefore with the Evangelist, that he was man; why are we not to believe the same Evangelist, who in subsequent words assures us, he was, prior to such state of humiliation, existent with the father? *He was made flesh:* and how is he, who hath shrined his divinity in the veil of manhood, to be otherwise denominated, than as man? Such humiliation of himself, while fashioned in the form and figure of a man, whatever degree of divinity he might
under

under that shade possess, would in historical detail characterise him as a man. Thus, Gen. 18. the three angels, one of whom is stiled the Lord, that is the immediate messenger or angel of the Lord, appearing in the form and substance of men, are stiled men. And, in the next chapter, of the angels, that in the assumed shape of men visited Lot, it is said; *and the men put forth their hands, and pulled Lot into the house to them, and shut the door.* Gen. 32. *A man* is said to have wrestled with Jacob: yet that man we learn was no other, than the angel of the Lord. *For Jacob called the name of that place Penuel ; because he had there seen God face to face.*

A second objection to this doctrine is urged in terms to the following purport. " If a divine being, ' in the instance of " Christ,' had really animated a human " body ; it must have appeared in the " course of his history, that such an ex- " traordinary measure was necessary." Now

Now I really fee not the neceffity of the confequence inferred. If the fact really were fo, I conclude it expedient and neceffary, that it fhould be fo; without feeing fuch neceffity in terms afferted. However it happens, for the fatisfaction of the objector; that the neceffity is abfolutely declared: though he has been fo unfortunate, as to overlook the declaration. *Him God raifed up, having loofed the pains of death, becaufe it was not poffible he fhould be holden of it.* Acts ii. 24. But if mere man, why not poffible? The abfolute impoffibility therefore being thus afferted, according to this writer's requifition, by his own argument proves our Lord's divinity.

It is further objected againft Chrift's divinity, that his apoftles are frequently reprefented as on a level with himfelf; and that many paffages of fcripture exprefsly fay, they will be advanced to fimilar, if not equal honour. Unfortunately however for the bold afferter of this

this extraordinary remark, the very paſſages, adduced by him in proof of ſuch equality, militate directly againſt it. Such are the following : *That they may be one ; as thou, father, art in me, and I in thee, that they may be one in us.* — *And the glory, which thou gaveſt me, I have given them ; that they may be one, even as we are one : I in them, and thou in me, that they may be made perfect in one ; and that the world may know that thou has ſent me, and haſt loved them, as thou haſt loved me.* The import of the petition is, " that " cloſely connected as he was with the " father in love and obedience, ſo his " diſciples might be in love and obedi- " ence to the father and him." The nature of the unity implied is further explained, in the ſubſequent clauſe *that they may be perfect εις εν, unto one thing*; " that they may unite in deſign and " operation to that one great end, the " redemption of mankind." And ſo far from declaring his diſciples on a level with himſelf, the words imply a
marked

marked inferiority to him : in as much as he, who gives glory, is superior to him, to whom he gives it. The glory, here spoken of, is the power of working miracles ; a power, which as the father had given him, he had exercised a similar authority, and given to his disciples, in testimony to the world, that he had received his commission from the father; and in proof that the father, in permitting that power to be delegated to them, had loved them, not in the same degree, but καθως, as, even as, manifestly as, *thou hast loved me.*

"Other parts of this remarkable "prayer, 'adds the author,' are in the "same strain." For the satisfaction of my audience I will subjoin some of those parts alluded to. *I have given unto them the words, which thou gavest to me: and they have received them, and have known surely, that I came out from thee, and they believed that thou hast sent me.* In this ejaculation how does our Lord here

SERMON VIII.

characterise his disciples? Not as immediately coming themselves from God; but as acknowledging him the immediate delegate of God, and knowing that he was so. Here is a manifest distinction observed between them: A distinction wide as the different degree of honour, in being the immediate delegate of God, come from the presence and a participation of the glory of the father, to reveal his will to men; and one of those, to whom such revelation was made, and who acknowledged it: a distinction obvious as the difference implied in receiving a kingdom, and being appointed to employs of honour in that kingdom under him, who received it.

1. Cor. 15. 24. Christ's kingdom is said to have an end: and from thence an argument is formed against his pre-existence. *Then cometh the end, when he shall have delivered up the kingdom to God, even the Father. And when all things shall be subdued unto him, then shall the Son also*

alſo himſelf be ſubject unto him, that put all things under him, that God may be all in all. " This, ' ſays the objector,' " is what we ſhould hardly have ex- " pected, if Chriſt had been the firſt of " all created Beings: by whom all " things were made, and who upholds " and governs all things." It is ſuffi- cient to draw up this argument in form, to expoſe the weakneſs of it. " If " Chriſt exiſted from the beginning of " his kingdom there could be no end. " But the ſcriptures aſſure us, that of " Chriſt's kingdom there will be an " end: therefore he could not have ex- " iſted from the beginning." How the termination of Chriſt's kingdom, erected on the redemption of mankind, ſhould depend on the date of his firſt exiſtence, it is not eaſy to conceive. When the œconomy of that redemption ſhall be completed, and Chriſt's mediatorial king- dom of courſe ceaſe: by no rule of rea- ſoning doth it follow, that Chriſt ſhall not continue to exiſt, accompanied with

every

Sermon VIII every appendage of universal sovereignty, in the plenary enjoyment of an eternal weight of Glory.

In proof of Chrift's abfolute and real humanity another argument is founded on a paffage in the epiftle to the Hebrews, which in our tranflation runs thus. *We see Jefus, who was made a little lower than the angels, for the suffering of death, crowned with glory and honour.* Heb. 2. 9. The original is, Τον δε βραχυ τι παρ' αγγελους ηλαττωμενον βλεπομεν Ιησουν, δια το παθημα του θανατου: and the literal tranflation, *for we see Jefus, who was for a little time leffened below the angels, for, or by, or on account of the suffering of death,* The word ηλαττωμενον is very fignificant of his pre-exiftence, and in a fuperior ftate. And the paffage not only proves, that, previous to his prefent humiliation, he did exift in a fuperior ftate; but in fome meafure afcertains the degree of fuperiority he poffeffed, viz. a ftate of nature above the angelic.

It

It alfo evinces the particular, in which he was leffened : not by any privation of his divinity, but in being fubjected to the fuffering of death, the angels enjoying a bleffed immortality.

To the fuppofition of Chrift having exifted in a prior ftate and fuperior ftation it is objected, that St. Luke mentions in him an *increafe of wifdom and ftature*: which, on fuch fuppofition, the objector finds a difficulty in reconciling to his idea. There may be a difficulty; but it is certainly fuch as implies no impoffibility. Let us therefore hear what fcripture fays in explanation of it.

The apoftle to the Philipians ch. ii. v. 6. obferves of Chrift, that εν μορφη Θεου υπαρχων, εαυτον εκενωσεν, μορφην δουλε λαβων. The word μορφη fignifies not only the external form or furface; but often the whole fubftance, and effential nature. And fuch is plainly the import of it in the

the paſſage before us: the word in any other ſenſe being unapplicable to God. According to this interpretation then of the word μορφη, the meaning of the paſſage is obvious: "who, when he was "of divine nature and eſſence, emptied "himſelf, that is, diveſted himſelf of "his glory, taking the nature of a ſer- "vant.

Let us next examine, how this paſſage of St. Paul correſponds with what the evangeliſt John hath ſaid on the ſame ſubject: for ſcripture is the beſt comment on ſcripture. John i. 1. Ὁ λογος ην προς τον Θεον, και Θεος ην ὁ λογος. — και ὁ λογος σαρξ εγενετο. *The word, that was with God, and that was God, was made,* or became, *fleſh*.

Now if the logos, which the Evangeliſt ſays *was God*, and the Apoſtle affirms to have been *of the nature and eſſence of God*, according to that Evangeliſt became, or *was made fleſh*, and according to to the Apoftle took the nature of man: he took with it all the infirmities and affections of human nature; and muft neceffarily have experienced the imbecility of infancy, and with maturing age an increafe of the powers of body and mind.

If it be queftioned, in the language of Chrift's fceptical vifitor, *how thefe things can be*; how fuch an abfolute converfion of the logos into manhood could be effected: with humble diffidence in our own capacity, let us ingenuoufly acknowledge we cannot explain it. But it hath been proved to be expreffly afferted: and where the affertion implies no impoffibility, I may on fufficient authority believe a fact, though I can neither explain, nor account for it. I have the affurance of an apoftle, that *great is the myftery of Godlinefs, God manifeft in the flefh*: as fuch I acknowledge it, without endeavouring to pry into fecrets, perhaps known only to God himfelf; and without prefuming, with the

SERMON VIII.

the key of human knowledge, to lay open that, which the spirit of God hath declared a mystery. Our present investigation is no farther concerned, than in proving it the doctrine of scripture. As such, other arguments, and another train of reasoning, will supply abundant proof that it is the doctrine of truth.

In vain presumption to fix the bounds, within which divinity may expose or conceal its nature, another argument against the divinity of Christ is urged from the improbability " of a man, who " died on the cross, having been the ma- " ker of the world." It is improbable too, that a Being, who, though in the appearance of man, was produced by the energetic influence of the holy spirit, and born without a human father; who could penetrate into the hidden secrets of mens hearts, who could control or suspend the powers of nature, bid the sea be still, and be obeyed, and by divesting himself of gravity, or giving a temporary solidity

to the water, walk upon the fwelling Sermon
furge; who could exercife even a crea- VIII.
tive power, in feeding feveral thoufand
people on fome morfels, in themfelves
infufficient to fatisfy a few individuals;
and laftly who, having died on a crofs,
after his burial revived, and in embodied
form and fubftance exercifed all the
functions of life, for the fpace of forty
days converfed freely with his friends,
and after that afcended openly before
them into heaven; it is improbable, that
he, who was poffeft of fuch powers as
thofe, fhould be that weak, impotent, limited being, a mere and abfolute man.

I will mention only one objection
more: which is founded on the argument from analogy. From the affumed
denial of the pre-exiftence of human
fouls, it is inferred that the foul of Chrift
could not have pre-exifted: analogy requiring, " that the whole human fpecies
" be upon one footing, in a cafe, which
" fo very nearly concerns the firft and
" confti-

SERMON "constituent principles of their nature."
VIII. It is freely confessed, that no argument
can be produced in proof of the pre-
existence of human souls: and on the
other hand it is equally clear, that no
argument of weight can be advanced
against the doctrine, except the want of
consciousness: a defect, as hath been
already observed, * from which the superior nature and mind of Christ were
free.

As to the pre-existence of human
souls, notwithstanding the many inge-
nious conjectures, that have been urged
in support of it, conceding to this writer
his full postulatum of its being a false
and erroneous doctrine; no argument
can be framed from the analogy of human
nature to that of Christ. The difference
of Christ's nature from that of mere
man, is the great point in controversy:
and to build an argument on the sup-

* See page 248.

posed

posed equality of them, is begging the question. What equality of nature is there in a mere man, and him, who was produced by the efficiency of the holy spirit, without a human father; between him, whose feeble powers are contained within narrow limits, and controled by positive laws, and him whose powers seemed to know no bounds, and, instead of submitting to, superseded the laws of nature; between him, whose body putrifies in the grave, and whose separated soul exists where the common course of mortality claims it, and him who triumphant over death rose from the grave, his soul not left in Hades, nor his body subjected to corruption? And in beings, wherein subsists so little equality, no argument can be founded on a supposed analogy: no, not even in the particular case, with which the argument we are now considering is qualified, " in the " first and constituent principles of na- " ture."

Such

SERMON VIII.

Such are the principal objections, I have in modern writers * observed, to the doctrine of the pre-existence and divinity of Christ: and to the objections of modern authors, on every subject in the course of the preceding lectures discussed, I have particularly applied myself. And now in a few words to press on you the subject of those discourses, let me observe; that, if there be a God, who made, and preserved us, and who will take account of our conduct, there must be such a duty as religion; and that it is both a serious, and a necessary thing: so serious, and so necessary, that as its regards extend to eternity, eternal happiness or misery attend our right election of, and correspondent conduct in it. Freely investigate it: examine the volume, in which as with the finger of God I think, and have supposed, it written. Though it may contain some

---

* Dr. Priestley, Mr. Lindsey, &c.

things

things hard to be underftood ; it holds forth much, that if practiced will improve our nature: enough fo chearing and intelligible, as to excite our endeavours to underftand it more and more. The doctrinal parts of religion are fcientific: and where is the fcience, that hath not its myfteries? The moft demonftrable of all fciences, even mathematics, has them.

Look through nature, as fhe lies before you in the works of this our world: and myftery meets the mind at every ftep. And will you extend your thoughts, beyond the confines of this habitable globe, to God, and a world to come; and not expect to find fome myftery there? Shall we reject as falfe whatever we cannot comprehend? To how narrow a compafs then fhall we reduce truth? Doth human reafon rank fo high: or is God fo level with the capacity of mankind? Shall we queftion his declarations, becaufe we cannot

accom-

SERMON VIII. accommodate to the fize of our minds the defign and propriety of them? Shall we faftidioufly refufe affent to what He hath been pleafed to reveal; becaufe He hath not revealed more? Or fhall we not rather with due gratitude and humility acknowledge the goodnefs of God, who hath by the revelation of Jefus Chrift revealed fo much: who hath condefcended to unveil the blaze of divine majefty in fuch degree, as to enable mankind acceptably to ferve Him; and fo far made known the nature of another world, as to quicken our exertions, amidft the various manfions there to attain to a ftation of blifs and glory, through the applied merits and mediation of the fame Jefus Chrift our Lord?

Such is the anchor of hope, we have in Chrift: and fuch in fum and fubftance the doctrine, which in anfwer to the words of my text the fcriptures dictate. It is not in the ability of man to mend

mend them *; nor shall human devices prevail in refining them. In plain legible characters, *they contain the words,* all the words, *of eternal life.*

SERMON VIII.

* See Lindsey's sequel to his apology page 119.

DE
STATU PARADISIACO.
CONCIO
IN ECCLESIA BEATÆ MARIÆ
APUD OXONIENSES
HABITA.

Ecclus. vii. 30.

Hoc tantum inveni ; quod Deus homines perfectos creavit, ipsi autem ratiocinia plurima invenerunt.

TERRARUM hic noster orbis, & quicquid in orbe viret, quicquid ultra hujusce mundi fines aut oculus assequi, aut mens deprehendere possit, Deum optimum maximum arguit : tanta sapientia, tanta ubique patet Potentia. O orbem fœlicem, summi artificis, omnibus absolutum numeris, opus ; cui herba quæque

Concio IX.

CONCIO IX. quæque leviffima, cui quicquid avium pecudumque ufquam invenitur, aut pulchritudinem aut ufum fuppetit! O hominum fœliciffimum genus; cui tot utilia, tot perpulchra ferviunt! At longe aliter fe res habet : tot tamque præclara et benevolentiæ et fapientiæ Dei argumenta malum multiforme inquinat. Morborum numerofa cohors, nec arte nec medicinâ depellenda, humana corpora obfidunt; animos pravi affectus deturpant: durâ adeo lege vivitur, ut *fœliciffimus ille, qui minus mifer.*

Quo fonte derivata mala hæc, ut dicuntur, tam naturalia, quam moralia, vitam humanam miferiis ærumnifque obruerunt: quo pacto homines fœlicitate exciderunt, quos fœlicitatis perfruendæ gratiâ in lucem evocavit Deus, et olim et nunc temporis variè contenditur. Hinc alii, quales funt Manichæi, omnipotentiâ Dei denegatâ, dæmonem alterum potentem quidem, fed malefuadum et maleficum, fingunt: cui ordinis per-

perturbatio cordi eſt. Quodcunque boni aut excogitavit, aut effecit Deus; ut hoc inquinet, illud ut miſſum faciat, hic malorum opifex pro viribus uſque laborat: et artis chymicæ ratione quaſi inverſâ, ut ex optimo quoque malum eruat, huic labor atque opus eſt.

Concio IX.

Alii potentiam Dei ſummam eſſe agnoſcunt, providentiam ejus omnino tollunt. Deum talem deſignant, cujus majeſtati rerum humanarum moderamen ne minime conveniret; cujus fœlicitas ne perfecta et continuata fieret, hujuſmodi curæ quam maxime obſtarent: naturæ divinæ æſtimatores pravi, quippe qui, uti de Epic. reis teſtatur Cicero, * verbis relinquunt, re auferunt Deos; nihil curare eos nec ſui, nec alieni, fingentes.

Ipſâ Dei exiſtentiâ prorſus ſublatâ, nodum alii audaciter reſolvunt. Si Deus ſit, ſicut hi ratiocinantur, ab operibus ſuis cur malum haud procul amovit?

Vid. Cic. de Nat. Deor.

Concio IX. Aut nequivit fane, aut noluit. Vel poteſtas ejus, vel benevolentia eſt finita: Ens vero, quoquo modo finitum, nequit eſſe vere et abſolute Deus. Ratiocinio igitur ſi huic aſſentiamur, rerum hic lucidus ordo nullo moderamine certo geritur; ſed fors omnia verſat.

Hiſce variis de mali origine hypotheſibus accedit altera; quæ naturam humanam ita eſſe comparatam affirmat, ut a malo ſeparari et ſejungi humanitatis fors omnino nequeat. Animis, hac veri ſpecie delinitis, malum quaſi de eſſentiâ hominis eſſe videtur; et crimina quæque miſericordiâ potius, quam pœnâ digna putantur. Hinc, non me malum! ſed me miſerum! clamare quiſque in promptu habet: hinc neminem confitentem habemus reum; dum peccata quiſque non ſua deflet, ſed quæ humana parum cavit natura. Hominum vero crimina in naturam humanam dum temere transferant; ne in authorem naturæ culpa ad extremum recidat, iſti parum cavent philoſophi.

Opi-

Opinionum, quas fupra memoravimus, prioribus tribus jam prætermiffis, ad refellendam hanc pofteriorem, quippe quæ neotericis quibufdam præcipue arridet, fententiam potius accingor.

Concio IX.

Hominum genus e creatoris fummi manibus, adeo appetens mali, adeo impotens benè beatèque vivendi, adeo imperfectum evafiffe fingunt hujufce fententiæ propugnatores; ut innocentiæ perfectæ et fœlicitatis ftatus nec fuerit unquam, nec fore poterit. Si vero Mofeos de Statu Paradifiaco, atque autorum ethnicorum de ætate aureâ, fcriptis quid veri infit; philofophorum iftorum hypothefis reipsâ refellitur: et, ratiocinii fui fundamine fublato, caffum ruit quodcunque fuper extruitur. Statum igitur naturæ innocentiæ et fœlicitatis effe ftatum, ac forte tali beatum hominum genus olim floruiffe, hac in concione contenditur: cujus tripliciter divifæ hæc norma fervabitur.

CONCIO IX. I. Quid de hominum conditione primâ mundi ætate, in sacris scripturis traditum accepimus, primò exponendum est.

II. Auctores profanos, tum poetas, tum philosophos, eadem suffragantes deinde proferam.

III. Hæc tandem dogmata de Statu Paradisiaco, ab antiquissimis scriptoribus tradita, rationi esse consentanea tertiò comprobabitur.

I. Sermonis itaque hujusce prædictam mihi servanti normam, quid de primigenâ hominum conditione, scriptura sacra tradit, primò investigandum est. Fabricationem ἐξημερινην depingens Moses, * hæc refert;

* In istâ narratione quædam esse parabolica, nonnulli existimant: alii etiam sermonem totum exemplar artificiosum esse volunt ad res veras explicandas: nempe naturæ primæ statum Paradisiacum, & ejusdem degenerationem, necnon humani generis novitatem. Alii quasi historiam summâ fide dignam, narrationem totam

sensu

refert; " Deus omnia, quæcunque fa- bricaverat, afpexit; et ecce omnia bona:" omnia nempe ad aſſequendum finem, cujus gratiâ creabantur, in fefe fat poteftatis habuerunt. Innocentiam primœvam, et mali originem hiftoricus idem divinus planè et enucleatè exponit. Porro ratio vitæ, quam parentes primi agebant, morum fimplicitatem et fecuritatem, ab innocentiâ omnino ortam, hifce verbis tradita, luculenter defignat. " Ambo " erant nudi Adam et uxor ipfius, neque " illos pudebat *." Naturam nempe ducem et magiſtram fecuti, nec labis ullius confcii, nulla veſtium involucra quærebant; neque iis vitio fuit nuditas, dum

CONCIO IX.

fenfu omnino ad literam expreſſo complectuntur. Explicatio quænam fit veriffima, hic loci non inveſtigandum duco: talem, qualis contenditur, extitiſſe ſtatum, degenerationem poftea contigiſſe, fententiæ utriufque propugnatores pariter agnofcunt.

* Hiſtorici facri fententiæ iſti hæc Platonis conferatur. Γυμνοι δε και αςρωτοι θυραυλητις τα πολλα ενιμοιτο, το γαρ των ωρων αυτοις αλυπον εκεκρατο.

imago

Concio IX. imago Dei, formâ humanâ eluceffens, peccato intaminata ftetit.

Neque his folis claufulis Statûs Paradifiaci dogma innititur: fcripturis facris excerptæ, fententiæ aliæ proferri poffent, quæ creationis mundi hiftoriam, ficut a Mofe traditam accepimus, non folùm innuere, fed plane affirmare naturæ humanæ perfectionem, fatis arguunt. Innocentiæ et fœlicitatis primorum parentum fidem apud Judæos fummam valuiffe hinc præcipue liquet; quod Apoftoli de forte iftâ beatâ, traditionibus acceptâ, Mofe luculenter expofitâ, prophetarum monitis munitâ, non obfcurè, dubitanter, et quafi ambagibus, fummâ vero cum fiduciâ, loquuntur: quippe quod pro certo ufque habebatur. Sententias huc fpectantes, in novo fœdere paffim difperfas, ut plurimas omittam; hæc Pauli verba hujufce dogmatis argumentum ampliffimum præbent. " Sicut uno homine " peccatum in mundum introivit, mors " quoque peccati causâ, &c." ac in eodem

eodem capite paulum infra, " ficut ho- Concio
minis unius inobedientiâ plurimi fiebant IX.
peccatores, &c." Quibus ex claufulis
Apoftolum, ut fatisfa&ionem Chrifti
omnes compleéti omnis ætatis homines
probaret, fœlicitatis primæ ja&uram non
modo nudè et fimplicitèr affirmare conftat ; hoc vero ex dogmate, quafi re cog-
nitâ et univerfim concefsâ, ad alias pro-
bationes progreditur. Sed in re apertif-
fimâ diutius cur immorandum ? Tum
fœlicitatem primævam, tum fælicitatis
iftius ja&uram, fcriptura facra fi alibi ufque taceret ; ad utramque probandam
prædi&æ folæ claufulæ abunde fufficiunt,
et quafi vim habent demonftrationis.
Sententias ergo fupra memoratas hæc, de
quâ jam concionamur, claudat. " Hoc
" tantum inveni, quod homines perfec-
" tos effinxit Deus ; ipfi autem ratioci-
" nia plurima invenerunt."

Claufulis iftis cæterifque plurimis,
quæ, idem fpe&antes, in fcripturis facris
inveniuntur, fibi invicem collatis ; hæc
dogmata

Concio IX.

dogmata fummatim exinde fequi habentur. Mundi origine primâ homines, uti alia fingula fapientiffimi et omnipotentis auctoris opera, perfecti creabantur. Appetitus fingulos, ad fœlicitatem affequendam, ad promovendam virtutem unicè fpectantes, et mutùo et amicè confpirantes, ratio gubernatrix adminiftravit Satis et ad fœlicitatem et ad virtutem valebant: dum hanc excolant, illâ fruuntur; hâc læsâ, illa amittitur. Libera benè beatèque vivendi datur poteftas; nulla imponitur neceffitas : cuique incoacta fua ftetit voluntas. Minus morigeros denique fe præbuerunt, imperium Dei repugnarunt, juffàque detrectarunt : Inobedientiæ fuæ pænas luebant. Hinc malum oritur ; et vires acquirens eundo, longè latèque ingruit. Hoc fonte derivata, clades omnigena ubique diffunditur; hinc, quicquid vitam humanam miferam aut infuavem reddit, quale quale infit amari, id totum accipit ; ferofque in nepotes defluens, contagii inftar, naturam humanam commutaffe

commutaffe videtur; immo, fi fas fit Concio
vera loqui, commutavit. I

II. Senfu fcripturæ facræ de primâ hominum conditione ita breviter expofito; quid de eâdem autores profani confcripferunt, fervato propofito, proximè inveftigandum eft: rerum enim antiquiffimarum, quæ in literis facris continentur, hiftoriam, apud omnes gentes, quamvis plerumque obfcuram, remanfiffe conftat. Cumque concionis noftræ norma claufulas ex fcriptoribus ethnicis plures, quàm in hujufce generis fcriptis commendat ufus, proferri poftulet; apud hunc conteffum me excufatum iri fpero. A philofophis igitur ac hiftoricis, quippe queis major quam poetis fides habetur, initium fumendum duco. Quos inter præcipuus Plutarchus, philofophus idem et hiftoricus, regionis cujufdam, notis Paradifi diftinctæ, nomine infularum beatarum defignatæ, defcriptionem exhibet: cui orbis terrarum portiuncula omnino

Concio IX. nino nulla nunc temporis convenit.* " Imbres, *inquit ille,* rari et amæni hìc " loci decidunt; dum venti molliter ſpi- " rantes, et rore quaſi alati, inſulam per- " vagentur: quibus efficitur, ut ſtudio et " labore nullo eliciti, omnigenæ herbæ " fructuſque jucundiſſimi ſuaptè naſcan- " tur." Deſcriptioni huic ſententiam proxime ſequentem hiſtoricus inſuper addit. " † Adeo ut fides uſque ad bar- " baros perlata firma eſt, illic campos " eſſe Elyſios, et beatorum ſedes quas " Homerus decantavit." Hinc de Paradiſo, ſive beatorum ſede quid ſenſit Plutarchus, quid etiam barbari ſenſere, liquet.

* Ομβροις δε χρωμεναι μετριοις σπανιως, τα δε πλειστα πνευμασι μαλακοις και δροσοβολοις, ου μονον αρουν και φυτευειν περιεχουσιν αγαθην και πιονα χωραν, αλλα και καρπον αυτοφυη φερουσιν, αποχρωντα πληθει και γλυκυτητι βοσκειν ανευ πονων και πραγματειας σχολαζοντα δημον.

PLUT. in Vit. Sert.

† Ωστι μεχρι των βαρβαρων διηχθαι πιστιν ισχυραν, αυτοθι το ηλυσιον ειναι πεδιον, και την των ευδαιμονων οικησιν, ην Ομηρος υμνησει. Ibid.

Eadem

Eadem fere, quæ de infulis fortunatis Plutarchus, de infulâ Toprobanâ afferit Diodorus Siculus : hoc infuper addito, nempe quod hujufce regionis incolæ expertem morborum vitam agebant. Nec prætermittendum duco, quod de morte Tobrobanitarum hiftoricus idem tradit : utpote fententiam haud omnino ifti diffimilem, quam fcriptores quidam Chriftiani de morte, vel potius e vitâ exceffu, in ftatu paradifiaco fi homines ufque permanfiffent, ftatuere. *" Duplex apud eos " nafcitur herba; cui fi quis indormiat, cru- " ciatûs omnis et doloris expertem mors " grata fuavifque fupervenit." Sententia ifta Diodori Mofaicæ *arboris vitæ* explicationem fortaffe veriffimam præbet ; quippe qua ab origine narratio illa primitùs derivatur. Mors, fi hiftorico facro fidem habeamus, non humanitatis conditio, fed peccati pœna, plane conftituta

{Concio IX.}

---

* Φυεσθαι γαρ χαυτοις διφυη βοτανην, εφ ης οταν τις κοιμηθη, λεληθοτως και απονως προς υπνον κατενεχθεις αποθνησκει. Diod. Sic. lib. 2.

fuit.

Concio IX. fuit. Arbori vitæ igitur talem quid vetat ineſſe vim, qualis ſructum ejus guſtanti tranſitum facilem atque ſuavem ad immortalitatem conciliaret?

Paradiſum quendam in Africâ ſitum Procopius fingit; fontibus amœnis irrigatum, ſylvis ornatum, viridantibus uſque, quæque uſque dulce redolebant: dum aerem tepentem frigiduli venti continuò mulcerent. Talem denique ſtatum, qualis hac in concione contenditur, olim revera extitiſſe, non ſolos inter Hebræos, aut Ægyptos, aut Græcos fides valuit; in idem conſentientes Indos quoque habemus: quos apud Calanus Alexandrum magnum ita alloquens a Strabone inducitur.* " Tritici hordeique olim

---

* Το παλαιον παντ' ην αλφιτων και αλευρων πληρη, καθαπερ και νυν κονιως· και κρηναι δ' ερρεον, αι μεν υδατος, γαλακτος δ' αλλαι, και ομοιως αι μεν μελιτος, αι δ' οινου, τινες δ' ελαιου· υπο πλησμονης δ' οι ανθρωποι και τρυφης εις υβριν εξεπισον. Ζευς δε, μισησας την καταστασιν, ηφανισε παντα, και δια πονου τον βιον απιδειξι. Strab. lib. 15.

" erant,

" erant, ficut nunc pulveris, omnia ple-
" na ; fontes quoque, alii aquâ, lacte alii,
" alii melle, alii vino, nonnulli oleo flue-
" bant : donec ob fatietatem luxuriamque
" homines in contumeliam fefe tradide-
" runt. Statum igitur præfentem Ju-
" piter exofus, omnia abolevit ; * *vitam-*
" *que labore degendam inftituit.*" Nemo,
ut opinor, hæe legens, quo ex fonte
manarint, diu dubitabit.

Scriptoribus iftis, regionem naturâ
plane eandem, fitu loci utcunque diver-
fam, defignantibus philofophum gravem
et inftar omnium Platonem jam tandem
liceat mihi fubjicere. In dialogo ifto,
cui titulus Πολιτικος adfcribitur, quippe
qui, prooemium veluti, libris fequentibus
Πολιτειας και νομων præponitur, de origine
politiæ philofophus fusè difserit. Et re
altè repetitâ, hominem a Deo creatum
conditione primâ beatiffimâ et verè aureâ

* Vid. Genef. Cap. 2 Com. 19.

potitum

Concio IX. potitum effe docet. Ætatis aureæ et fælicis defcriptionem μυθον appellat; traditionem aliunde defumptam ifto nomine defignans: ne quis forfan pro figmento et fomniis quafi φιλοσοφῶντος narrationem habeat. Fidem ac authoritatem quam huic μυθῳ conciliatam vellet, hæc fua teftantur verba.* " Ifta nobis tradiderunt primi
" illi majorum noftrorum, qui primam
" mundi revolutionem proxime contingebant. Horum fermonum teftes præco"nefque illi extiterunt." Platonicæ ifti primævæ fœlicitatis tabellæ, coloribus adeo vividis depictæ, haud abs re erit paulò diutius immorari: in qua fi veritatem ipfam non deprehendamus, veritatis faltem veftigia nemo fere non agnofcet. †" Ætate ifta, nihil erat ferum;
" neque

---

* Απεμνημονευετο δ' υπο των ημετερων προγονων των πρωτων, οι τελευτωσῃ μεν τη προτερα περιφορα τον εξης χρονον εγειτονουν, της δε κατ' αρχας εφυοντο. Τουτων γαρ ουτοι κηρυκες εγενονθ' ημιν των λογων. Plato Πολιτ:

† Τοτε ουκ αγριον ουδεν, ουτε αλληλων εδωδαι, πολεμος ουκ ενην, ουδε ςασις τοπαραπαν. — Θεος ενεμεν αυτους, αυτος

επιςτατων.

" neque aliæ alias animantes vorabant: Concio
" aberat bellum penitus atque feditio. IX.
" ——Deus homines pafcebat; ipfe erat
" et paftor eorum et cuftos: ipfoque
" eos regente, civitatum conftitutiones
" nullæ extabant.——Fructus illis, et
" poma et fruges, arbores et fertile folum
" fponte fuâ fubminiftrabant." De Saturni regno alia plurima philofophus idem fcribit; quæ ftatum paradifiacum quam veriffime defignant. Alia, ut ipfe teftatur, innumera, et illis longe mirabiliora, ab ejufdem μυθου quafi fonte permanant: longinquitate vero temporis, partim funt exoleta, partim difperfa atque diffipata perturbate dicuntur.

Defcriptioni illi uberrimæ fi quid amplius deerit, quo Platonis fententia de hac re plenius enitefceret; Τιμαια, five περι φυσεως dialogi, pars ifta, in quâ de hominum creatione agitur, argumenta huc

επιςτατων.—Νεμοντος δε εκεινου. πολιτειαι ουκ ησαν.—Καρπους δε αφθονους ειχον απο τε δρυων και πολλης υλης αλλης, ουκ υπο γεωργιας φυομενους, αλλ' αυτοματης αναδιδουσης της γης. Plat. ibid.

T   fpec-

Concio IX. fpectantia ampliſſima præbet ; ubi de mali causá et origine argutè diſſeritur. Ex involucris tandem, quibus veritas fere obruitur, hoc veri erui poteſt : homines benè, juſtè, et honeſtè vixiſſe contenditur, dum in femet impreſſam dei ſimilitudinem puram atque intaminatam conſervarent ; malè vero, poſtquam cupiditatibus craſſis et corporeis femet ipſos involviſſent.

Ab hiſtoricis et philoſophis ad poetas deſcendere, ac Homerum Elyſios campos depingentem in primis audire, erit operæ pretium.

> Vitæ hic humanæ ratio jucunda paratur ;
> Nec fera tempeſtas, nec nigri nubila cæli
> Inficiunt æthram, tranquillâ luce ſerenam :
> Suaviter aſt Zephyri ſpirantes arva ſalutant,
> Et leviter ſtringunt recreata ſilentia ponti. *

Quid de hortis Alcinoi dicam ? Nonne et hi et illi ab eodem fonte derivan-

---
* Τη περ ενιςτη βιοτη πιλει ανθρωποισι,
Ου νιφετι, ουτ' αρ' χειμων πολυς, ουτι ποτ' ομβρος.
Αλλ' αιει ζεφυροιο λιγυπνειοντας αητας
Ωκεανος ανιησιν αναψυχειν ανθρωπους.

tur ?

tur? Vana omnino fictaque cecinisse Concio poetam grex totus criticorum negat. IX. Quó vero pictura illa amœni, immo amœnitatis, horti referenda est? Non, ut iidem fingunt, ad infulas Atlanticas; neque ufquam regionum præter eam, ab hominibus primis enarratam, a primis fcriptoribus depictam, præter Paradifum.

Genus hominum primigenorum decantans, locum Homero proximum Hefiodus fibi vendicat; ejufdem, ut aliqui volunt, ut alii, ætatis prioris fcriptor.

Tunc homines divûm vivebant more; neque illos
Anxia curarum moles, operumque labores
Laffabant: aberat morbus, triftifque Senectus.
Igneus aft ollis vigor; et dum corpore vires
Regnabant folido, convivia læta placebant.
Mors fimilis fomno fuit, atque uberrima tellus
Omnia liberius nullo cogente ferebat
In commune bonum, nec quifquam invidit habenti. *

* Ὥστε θεοὶ δ' ἱζωον ακηδεα θυμον εχοντες
Νοσφιν ατερτε πονων και οϊζυος· ουδε τι διλον

Nemo,

Concio IX.

Nemo, ut opinor, scriptorum Christianorum statum Paradisiacum plenius et melius depinxit, quám in istis versibus Hesiodus. Ætatem auream ab Ovidio in libro primo metamorphosium expressam, utpote omnibus notam, praetermitto. Neque de regno Saturnio tacet Virgilius :

> Ante jovem nulli subigebant arva coloni :
> Nec signare quidem, aut partiri limite campum
> Fas erat ; in medium quærebant : ipsaque tellus
> Omnia liberius, nullo poscente, ferebat.

Ad calcem libri proxime sequentis scilicet secundi Georgicorum, hi versus idem quoque spectant.

> Ante etiam sceptrum Dictæi regis, et ante
> Impia quàm cæsis gens est epulata iuvencis ;
> Aureus hanc vitam in terris Saturnus agebat.

> Γηρας επην· αιει δε ποδας και χειρας ομοιοι
> Τερπουτ' εν θαλιησι, κακων εκτοςθεν απαντων.
> Θνησκον δ' ως υπνω δεδμημενοι· εσθλα δε παντα
> Τοισιν ην· καρπον εφερε ζειδωρος αρουρα.
> Αυτοματη, πολλοντε, και αφθονον, &c.
>
> Hes. Εργ. Και Ημερ.

En

PARADISIACO. 293

En manifeftam ftatûs Paradifiaci notam : Concio
quum homines nondum animalium car- IX.
ne, fed folis terræ fructibus vefcerentur !
Sententiæ iftæ variæ, ex fcriptoribus antiquis excerptæ, fuaviloquis hifce verbis
Lucretianis jam tandem claudentur.

Iamque adeo affecta eft ætas, affœtaque tellus,
Vix animalia parva creat, quæ cuncta creavit
Sæcla, deditque ferarum ingentia corpora partu.

Præterea nitidas fruges, vinetaque læta
Sponte fuâ primum mortalibus ipfa creavit.
Ipfa dedit dulces fœtus, et pabula læta :
Quæ nunc vix noftro grandefcunt aucta labore.

Statum hominum primigenium eo, quo
nunc degitur, perfectiorem ecce ipfum
Epicuri difcipulum plane agnofcentem
habemus. Neque ftatum naturæ talem
poeta ifte agnoviffet, nifi ut rem fide dig-
niffimam : rem univerfâ traditione ac-
ceptam, graviffimorum hominum aucto-
ritate fancitam. Narrationes igitur iftas,
quibus ipfe Lucretius fuffragatur, pro
anili

Concio IX.

anili fabellâ ecquis ducet? Scriptorem illum, qui animum fabulis vanis arctifque religionis compagibus occupatum exfolvere jactat, illum inquam credulitatis arguere, ecquis in animum inducat?

De ftatu Paradifiaco quæ tot tantique fcriptores protulerunt, alii penè innumeri, fi res poftularet, et locus ferret, eadem fuffragantes allegari poffent. Quid, ifta omnia de conditione hominum primigeniâ pro figmentis poeticis habenda putabimus? Nonne philofophos, nonne hiftoricos, viros eruditos graviffimofque in eadem confentientes habemus: fingulos, fi non vera, certe verifimilia proferentes? Atque iftas fingulas de regno Saturni, ætate aureâ, et fimilibus defcriptiones, obumbratas quidem et variis erroribus implicitas, hiftoriæ Mofaicæ veftigiis infiftere et infequi nullus dubito. Ab extremo fonte, nempe a primævis hominibus derivatas, veriffimas ætatis primæ narrationes accepit

cepit Noa : eafdemque, a Noæ filiis tra- Concio
ditas, pofteros accepiffe, conftat. * IX.

III. Tertiò probandum reftat, ut hiftoriæ iftæ de Statu Paradifiaco, a primis hominibus acceptæ, fcriptoribus tum facris, tum profanis confirmatæ, minimé futiles effe et ineptæ demonftrentur : immo e contra, rationi confentanea, naturâ humanâ digna, Deo optimo maximo digniffima effe hypothefis ifta contenditur. Omne ens, ut loquuntur fcholaftici, eft perfectum : quo dogmate perfectio relativa, non abfoluta, fignificatur. Quodcunque a fapientiffimo Deo creatum eft, id omnibus numeris abfolutum creari neceffe eft : dum fingulæ cujufque animantis facultates atque organa, inopiis fuis fubveniendis, fuis optatis potiundis aptæ et idoneæ, fœlicitati propriæ infer-

* Primam hominis vitam cum fimplicitate fuiffe, et nudo corpore, docebant et Ægyptii ; unde aurea poetarum ætas, etiam Indis celebrata, ut apud Strabonem eft. Grotius de ver Rel. Chr. lib. 1. Sect. 16.

viant,

Concio IX.

viant, ad fœlicitatem propriam affequendam omnino fufficiant. Hoc experientia docet omnium, qui in ftudiis hiftoriæ phyficæ verfantur : hoc, quaquaverfum oculos circumferamus, adeo conftat ; ut fi Davidi liceat jure exclamare, ' *O Domine, in fapientiâ omnia fecifti :* haud injuriâ exclamationem alteram fubjecit, *terra, O Domine, plena eft benevolentiâ tuâ.*

O infœlicem humanæ naturæ fortem, O homines infortunatos : qui, hujufce orbis dominatores conftituti, in hoc orbe miferi foli deprehenduntur ; qui tot animalium principes, uniufcujufque fua quatenus poftulat natura perfecti, imperfecti foli effinguntur ! Cuinam enim bono dux ifta et jucundiffima comes vitæ, ut vanè garriunt philofophi, ratio infervit ? Quapropter divinæ ifta auræ particula nobis conceffa eft ? Anne, ut perfectionis iftius, iftius virtutis apicem hominibus oftendat, quem natura humana nequit attingere ; anne ob ea ut excruciet homines, quæ hominum natura effugere nequit,

nequit, commissa ; anne ut miseros homines reddat ? *Talia, O Domine, procul tibi absint consilia!* Actionum ergo humanarum moderatrix ista conceditur, ut actiones morales dirigat, ut appetitus cohibeat, ut vitam suavem atque jucundam reddat. Ei itaque assequendo fini aut sufficit ratio, aut non. Si non, impar est fini instituto ; ac homines, quibus hujusce finis gratiâ ratio conceditur, eatenus sunt imperfecti : Omne vero ens e manibus creatoris perfectum evasit. Fini igitur proposito sufficit ratio : nunc autem temporis fini isti rationem haudquaquam sufficere experientia quotidiana testatur ; ergo olim se rem ita habuisse necesse est. Atque ex his ratiociniis sequitur, talem fuisse primævum naturæ humanæ statum, qualem a primis scriptoribus expressum accepimus.

Concio IX.

Quantum miseriarum vitam hominum obsidet, neminem latet : ac prævidentia ipsa miseriarum quæ eludi nequeunt,

quas

Concio IX. quas neque prudentia effugere, neque ipsa virtus repellere valet, ærumnas istas graviores reddit. Ferarum vita in malis versatur; illas vero nec præteriti recordatio, neque timor futuri excruciatas tenet; natura illis largita est jucunda oblivia vitæ. Ast morbi, dolores, mors, et pallida malorum cohors, non modo hominum vestigia comites certissimi insequuntur, oculis autem continuo obversantur, et mentibus quasi inhærent. Et si partem alteram vitæ humanæ, lucidam nempe et splendidiorem, contemplemur, certa homines ne minima quidem voluptas manet. Hoccine vero creatoris benevolentis, hoccine est Dei optimi maximi; ut animantes crearet, quas magna et plurima necessario premunt mala; quarum vitas voluptates parvulæ tantum, breves, et fortuitæ mulcent?

Quid, nonne hominis vita, affectibus cum ratione bellum civile gerentibus, certamine perpetuo versatur? Meliora laudare atque probare, deteriora sequi,

humanum

humanum eſt. Spes, Timor, Ira, Grex totus affectuum ασυνταξιαν ciens, viciſſim dominatur; dum ratio, gubernatrix veluti timida et puſilla, ſervis iſtis rebellibus politiam hominis internam adminiſtrandam tradit. Facultatum hanc humanarum dominam et reginam, quid verum eſt atque decens monentem, homines male adverſantur : iis, prava jubentibus, aures faciles præbent ; qnodcunque mali conſuiunt, obtemperare heu nimis parati! Hebeſcentibus denique et quaſi defatigatis appetitibus torva aſpici redit ratio ; delictique nos tunc ſerò pudet, piget, pœnitetque. Quid multis ? Peccare, et pœnitere, atque iterum peccare, vitam humanam miſerâ viciſſitudine diſtinguit.

CONCIO IX.

Humani generis Picturæ tali tabellam alteram et longè diverſam jam tandem conferre liceat : hominis imaginem, innocentiæ et fœlicitatis compotem. Corporis atque animi vires puta aptè amicèque conſpirantes : mentem ſcientiâ omnigenâ inſtructam ; arbitrium voluntati

Dei

Concio IX. Dei inferviens; appetitus congrua et confentanea quærentes, affectus denique fummiſſos et rationi obtemperantes: facultatibus humanis ita ordinatis, (et facultates recte ordinari quid vetat?) harmonia Platonica inde fequitur: hinc Mofeos Status Paradifiacus; hinc ætas aurea poetarum.

Perfectionis iſtius apicem, in qua homines primitus creari demonſtrat ratio, ipforumque conditionem, quam experientia hodierna probat, qui perpenderunt philofophi, tantæ metamorphofeos caufas hinc et inde quæfiverunt. Quin talis effecta fuit Morum atque Indolis Mutatio, nemo fere dubitavit; caufa ufque latebat. Nodum iſtum refolvere, nodum herclè Deo vindice dignum, veritatis fons et principium Deus ipfe dignatus eſt: *Nubefque inter et tenebras, quæ obvolvunt cum, æquitatem et juſtitiam folo ejus infidere, demonſtravit.* Et ecquis adeo iniquus eſt rerum æſtimator, qui œconomiæ divinæ explicationem talem nullius ponderis aut

aut usûs leviufculi pendit ? At nihilne intereft, ut de Deo et nobis ipfis recte fentiamus ? Nihilne intereft, ut nobis innotefcat, quam ob culpam in hunc mundum, veluti in carcerem, Deus homines relegavit; miferiis innumeris obfitos, fœlicitatis veræ vix umbris relevatos? Hæc denique nefcientibus, fœlicitatem eorum futuram ecquæ argumenta compertam facient? Si hic mifer fim, et id unde fiat, nefcio; quomodo fciam me non pofthac quoque miferum futurum? Dubitationes iftas curafque follicitas, quibus tenetur quifque cui fua fœlicitas cordi eft, Deus jam benignè diffipavit; et formidinis loco fpes novas fuppeditavit. Verbum igitur Dei, in fcripturis facris quafi jubare confcriptum, in queis reteguntur arcana, mundi ab origine primâ caliginofi erroris nebulis obvoluta, in queis folummodó falus, in queis nuda fimplexque veritas deprehenditur, animo facili gratoque amplecti, noftrum eft. Hoc duce ufa, vires novas ratio

Concio IX.

Concio IX. ratio depromet; quæ, fi male faftidiofa ducem fequi dedignetur, in errorum turbine tumultuante illico immergitur: quo fit, ut nihil ferè adeo abfurdum inveniatur, quod non aliquis θεολογ8ντων nofftratum affeveravit.

FINIS.